T0196498

TO WALK HUMBLY WITH GOD

The Carroll Kakac Story

STEVEN LEE

WESTBOW
P R E S S®
A DIVISION OF THOMAS NELSON
& ZONDERVAN

THE HOLY BIBLE, NEW INTERNATIONAL VERSION®, NIV® Copyright © 1973, 1978, 1984, 2011 by Biblica, Inc.® Used by permission. All rights reserved worldwide.

WestBow Press books may be ordered through booksellers or by contacting:

WestBow Press
A Division of Thomas Nelson & Zondervan
1663 Liberty Drive
Bloomington, IN 47403
www.westbowpress.com
1 (866) 928-1240

ISBN: 978-1-5127-6423-9 (sc)
ISBN: 978-1-5127-6422-2 (e)

Library of Congress Control Number: 2016919118

Print information available on the last page.

WestBow Press rev. date: 02/10/2017

TABLE OF CONTENTS

FOREWORD

"He has shown you, O mortal, what is good. And what does the Lord require of you? To act justly and to love mercy and to walk humbly with your God."

Micah 6: 8 NIV

Many people have thought it should be done, including me, but no one until now has attempted to capture in printed words the Carroll Kakac story. It is no wonder that no one has tackled it before.

Consider the U. S. capital building in all its awesomeness. We look at its image as a monument to liberty, freedom, perseverance, and virtue, yet the thought of planning and erecting such a building boggles the mind. We step back and say we are not equal to the task.

This is how I felt in 2013 at the prospect of writing a book about the minister to ministers, Carroll Kakac, whom I have known as pastor, friend, and mentor since the fall of 1970.

For several years, I felt that someone should write a book about him. No one was doing it, so I decided the writer would be me, for time was flying.

As with all my projects, I needed a plan of action. I decided to interview Carroll and to try to tell his story in his own words, the only thing missing being his voice, his facial expressions, and his gestures. Printed words are a poor substitute for spoken words, but by using direct quotations, primarily, I felt I could give as accurate a picture of Carroll as is possible.

What strikes me about Carroll—and always has—is his humility, his conviction that what he has done he has not done himself, that God has worked through him, and that God should have the glory for the things accomplished, not him. He sees himself only as an instrument that God has spoken through and has done victorious things through. The instrument, he believes, is only an incidental conduit, not a glorious thing in itself. Like the aqueducts of ancient Rome, Carroll sees himself as the means by which God has carried forth the gospel message. Carroll views himself as the aqueduct carrying the water of life, but not as the water itself. That's humility. He wants to be sure in his life that credit is given where it is due: to God, the Father.

The story of Carroll's life has some defining moments, some positive and some negative, after which nothing is the same as before for him and his family. With little consciousness of it, Carroll has also been part of many defining moments for others, especially so in leading them to accept Christ, in offering sage advice, and in being a strong, unflappable, and Christian example to people through the decades.

I ask you, reader, who has done more while shunning all praise for it?

From 1970 through 2002, Carroll had hundreds of weddings at which Kent Reeves and I played the music. He used to kid us and say that we "should take this show on the road." Also, he would say, "Now I'm not a talented person, so talented people have to help me." What an undervaluation. In everything, Carroll has been a rock—that takes talent, and lots of it. Dealing with people without making them upset or deluded takes infinitely more talent than playing music. Carroll has always had the right greeting, the right approach, the right answer, and the right advice: this book will solidly prove this.

Writing this book—which, at the start, seemed formidable, if not impossible—has been a privilege and a joy for me. And now I hand it over to you, reader, to learn more about my friend, Carroll Kakac, in his own words.

Steven Lee
February 9, 2017

Chapter 1

FAMILY AND HOME

I, Carroll Kakac, wasn't born with a silver spoon in my mouth on July 24, 1929, but I did enter the comfortable, established surroundings of a farm in Cresco, Iowa. Welcoming me were my parents, Victor Otto, 31, and Blanche Frazier Kakac, 29, and two brothers, Victor Otto and Fillmore Frazier. I was the namesake of Carroll Cole, my mother's cousin, an attorney in Lincoln, Nebraska. Later another brother and a sister, Don and Janice, joined us. So, I grew up as the middle child of 5 children.

Although the farm was fairly self-sufficient, three months after my birth, the stock market crashed, ushering in 10 years of economic depression. Money was scarce when I was little during the Great Depression. I remember getting a dime from the tooth fairy and a quarter a week allowance. A nickel could buy pop, a candy bar, or gum, and a movie ticket was a quarter. However, my family usually entertained ourselves at home. We grew up playing board games, like checkers and Monopoly, with our parents. My favorite birthday present was a jack knife my dad gave me. I still have a scar from cutting myself with it. My absolute favorite toy was a little red truck that a neighbor boy stole from me.

When I was growing up, people said I was short like Grandpa Frazier, but I had many of my mother's features. I was so short, in fact, that I was teased because my younger brother, Don, was taller than I was; I even had to wear his hand-me-downs.

Very aware of my heritage in these formative years, I loved to hear the stories about how Frantisek Kakac got to Iowa from Czechoslovakia. To this day I have always wanted to go to the Czech Republic. I made it as far as France once, but I developed some medical issues and couldn't complete that leg of my trip.

The Kakac family did get around some. Every summer we would go to Alexandria, Minnesota, to visit relatives and to fish. I clearly remember going there in our 1940 Ford when I was 10.

At home, Mom had a Maytag gas motor washing machine, an electric stove, a Zenith radio, and a coal-burning furnace. To keep cool in hot weather, we opened the windows. Seven of us lived in our house, and when we were all together, we laughed a lot. Also, our door was always open for friends and relatives. In fact, Mom said she never knew who would be there in the morning.

All of us had chores to do every day before and after school, We milked 18 to 20 cows and tended chickens and sheep.

My best friend was Walter Block, a neighbor my age, and my favorite pet was a dog named Prince.

Most kids at least think about running away from home. My dad told me if I wanted to leave home, he would give me the money to go wherever I wanted to go but not the money to get back. So, when I got angry or discontented, I would just walk on the road in back of our house, but I was seldom walking back there.

I was greatly influenced by Jack Dray, an old neighbor whom I visited very day, and my parents. To be a minister, I was most influenced by Mr. Lincoln, a businessman who sold Allis Chalmers tractors; he urged me to become a preacher. He challenged me to go to Bible college. While I was in high school, he and my speech teacher gave me the courage to go on and try.

Beyond home, Mom was in a local women's club, and Dad enjoyed playing in bands. My father could play multiple instruments and the Kakac family was known as a musical family. Unfortunately, I can't carry a tune in a bucket.

Holidays were pretty predictable. On Thanksgiving, we would have a feast. We would try to have the corn out of the field before that day, but sometimes we had to pick corn on that day. Halloween was so different then; I rarely dressed up, yet I did go out with friends and tip stuff over. On Christmas, we opened presents in the morning and went to Grandfather and Grandmother Frazier's for dinner. I usually got new clothes, school supplies, and money from my dad's sisters.

Life was so different then. For example, we had a party-line telephone, with several families on the same line. You could listen in on other families' conversations if you wanted to. But we did not excessively use the telephone like people do today. When I was 16, I learned to drive our 1940 Ford, paying a quarter for a license that didn't even require a test.

Of course, I lived in a part of Iowa where there was lots of snow. In shop class in high school, we learned how to build skis. When the snow came in the fall, we kind of stayed on the farm all winter long. And my dad was going to show us how to ski because he had grown up on that type of thing. We had a hill in our back yard. He got up at the top of the hill and started down and somehow fell, getting his back out of shape, and the rest of the winter he was laid up with back trouble. That was the first and last lesson on skiing I ever had. I found out that the old timers in Iowa to learn how to ski put a young person on skis and gave him two buckets half full of water in each hand and told him not to spill the water, and he would learn to ski in no time at all, holding up those buckets of water. I don't think skiing is part of the culture in Iowa anymore; maybe the weather is getting warmer.

School was certainly different, too, a school of one room with all eight grades in it. We made our own Valentines and exchanged them. My favorite class was usually math, and my least favorite was English, which I felt I didn't have a gift for. Miss Glennie, who gave me books to read, was my favorite teacher, and some said I was the pet, but, after all, she was my aunt. Walking one and a half miles to school each day, I never missed a day.

In high school, I was in band, playing a baritone, and in Future Farmers of America, but I never played athletics. At that time we did not have school dances. At graduation, I was chosen by my class to give the graduation speech. I think I was well-liked and happy. When we lined up by height for graduation, I was next to the shortest boy.

My first true love was Ardell Zaiser, who was really pretty and admired by several, but she liked me best. However, my mother warned me that "Bobbi" as she was known was, in fact, a distant cousin.

During my teenage years, our family was a happy one. We had lots of friends from the community and from the church youth group.

Without a doubt, the most memorable even in my life was becoming a Christian at the Church of Christ in Missouri Valley, Iowa. I remember walking down the sidewalk after I was baptized, thinking, "My sins are forgiven."

When my family got started back to church and when I became a Christian in high school, right from the beginning I was challenged to become a minister, but I made up my mind during a family reunion in Minnesota where we stayed for a week on a lake. It had been a very peaceful spiritual week for me in the midst of great natural beauty. One night I noticed the people were drinking and carrying on and maybe getting a little crazy. I made up my mind right then and there that I wanted to be a minister. They were thinking they were having fun but somehow I felt deep down they really weren't. Somehow it crystallized for me about what was really important in life.

Respect seems to be in short supply now. As an adolescent, I most respected my parents. As an adult, I most respected Mr. Earl Hargrove of Lincoln Bible Institute. These people had good values and at that time it was widely recognized by society that people such as this deserved respect and were to be emulated.

How my parents met, where they came from, and how we became Christians makes for an interesting story. My mother was a schoolteacher. A school teacher could take a test and become a teacher without ever going to college a day back then. Despite this, there were some incredible teachers.

Near Missouri Valley, Iowa, Dad was working with a friend in an orchard, which was right across the road from the school where Mother taught. She went to get her mail and met Dad for the first time at the mailbox.

The school I attended for eight grades had been built by my great grandfather Frazier, who donated the school and the cemetery to the community. He had also taught at that school.

My parents were married at the courthouse in Missouri Valley; afterwards they went back to where my dad came from, Cresco, Iowa. This is where their first 3 kids, including me, were born. Dad had an orchard and a greenhouse for several years. My father had attended Iowa State University in Ames, Iowa, and received a degree in horticulture. He also played on the football team for Iowa State but it wasn't nearly as big a deal back then as it is now. The Kakac family always placed a high value on education and a lot of us attended college at a time when it wasn't nearly as common, especially in farming communities.

There were two reasons that Dad got out of the orchard business. On November ll, 1940, a blizzard struck Missouri Valley, Iowa, Nebraska, and up into Wisconsin. In those days there was no way to forecast bad weather or to give people any forewarning.

It was during duck hunting season, and it had been an unusual fall, with leaves still on the trees; the temperature was 60 that morning and by midnight it was 25 below. Because the sap wasn't down in the trees yet, it killed every apple tree in the state. Dad didn't want to plant it over, for it would be 10 or 15 years before again producing.

The night of blizzard, duck hunters were not prepared with the right clothes; some got under their boats with dogs, but more than a hundred died. The Missouri River ran nearby our farm, and it was also the main flyway out of Canada for geese. Hunting was limited to 20 geese then. So, the reasons Dad got out of the orchard business were mainly the blizzard killed all the trees but also the memory of the duck hunters dying.

Grandma Frazier, my mother's mother, wanted the family to come back to Missouri Valley after Grandpa quit farming.

Grandpa Frazier had ordered a Sears Roebuck home from a catalogue about 1900. It was delivered by the Chicago-Northwest Railroad. Since the tracks ran right through Grandpa's land, they just stopped the train and unloaded all the components of the house, which were then hauled by horse and wagon up to the construction site. The house included everything: furniture, wall paper, 2 bathrooms. When my grandfather homesteaded there, it was 27 miles to nearest post office. The first winter there, they lived in a log cabin abandoned by Mormons. They built the first frame house in Western Iowa.

Great grandpa Frazier had come to Iowa in the 1840's and bought 540 acres of land at $1.25 per acre. My great-grandfather had enough money to buy his farm of 540 acres; Aunt Lucille always wondered how he could have all that money, which was over $1,000. My Frazier great-grandparents traveled to Iowa with the Mormons who were going west.

Grandpa's farm had the Big House, where we eventually lived—the one from Sears—and the Little House, which was the family home first built there. My sister, Janice, was born there.

Nearby was a house where three people had died from tuberculosis. Grandma would never allow us to go there for fear of contracting the disease. After the last family died in that house, it was burned to the ground to be on the safe side.

I went to a one-room school for the first eight grades and took a test after graduating to see if I could go on to high school or not. I graduated at the head of my class, the only one in it. We had two farms, and when we got home from school, we kids had to do the chores while Dad was at our other farm.

We were never hungry, we had plenty of clothes, and in the summer we didn't wear shoes. No one had any money. My folks would take milk and cream to town and trade them for flour and sugar. Mom canned all summer.

After I graduated from Missouri Valley High School, I thought I would be a farmer. However, during high school when all my family was baptized, that made me want to become a preacher. I never knew for sure if I could be a successful preacher, and still don't. In those days there was still a draft although no war going on, and I was drafted.

In 1948, I was drafted into the Army for 2 years; the U. S. still had the draft even though no war was going on then.

My Army time came along between WWII and the Korean War. We weren't in combat with anyone in the world, but we still had the draft. My name came out in the paper that I had been drafted and when to report. That's how people were notified of military service at that time.

A recruiting sergeant said he could get me into field artillery for 2 years. He said that if I got in field artillery, I would never have to walk. I signed up and when I said, " I do," they forgot about all the promises. No, we didn't walk; we ran. Miles and miles.

I was part of the 129th field artillery, a distinguished group out of Fort Leonard Wood, MO. We went around doing 21 gun salutes. I have no war stories to tell, for it was actually kind of like a vacation, compared to the farm work I was used to. At 6 a. m., we went out and did calisthenics, ate a nice breakfast, and then did work around the camp. We were about 300 miles from home. Sometimes my folks came down, for we had weekends off. I didn't have a bad experience. I was paid $30 a month in cash and sent part of it home. They gave me all my clothes. All 4 of us boys were in the Army.

The military unit I was in, the field artillery, was President Truman's unit from WWI, and we just went around places like Independence, Missouri, firing guns. Our captain said that anytime two guards would get into a fight, they would call in the 129th Field Artillery Battalion. Sometimes I wondered if we could fight our way out of a wet paper bag. But I'm sure all soldiers felt like that at times, and then were later surprised at what they could actually do. We mostly transported and fired big guns, which we could pull behind a truck, on wheels.

When I got out of the Army, I went to Lincoln Bible Institute, with the help of Brother John Boldon. For the baccalaureate, seniors chose the speaker, and they chose me. Previously the speaker had been a graduate, not a student. I did the baccalaureate for my own class.

Well, the school became a bit apprehensive, so they assigned me to a professor whose job it was to approve the sermon, and the only time I could preach the sermon to him was while he was working in his garden.

I can remember, I was a little aggravated with the professor who just kept on working. I said, "What if Jesus comes while you are working in the garden?" and he said, "He wouldn't dare come until I finished hoeing this row of beans."

I was president of the class, and I was editor of the yearbook. The only reason I took the yearbook job was because a shy, retiring man said, "If you take the job, I'll do the work," and that's the way we did it. I didn't have the background for it.

In 1944, Grandpa Frazier died, and Grandma wanted to set me up in farming with land and machinery already in place. Grandpa had died the same year we learned about my brother, Victor's, death in France, and Grandma always said that Grandmpa loved Victor so much—in fact, he loved all of us—that he just couldn't go on living. We went to Grandpa and Grandma's house every Sunday like clockwork for many years. They loved us, and we all knew that.

Surprising to many people, I was not born into a church-going family. My grandparents never went to church, but they did listen to religious programs on the radio. My Great-Grandpa Frazier had been an elder in the Church of Christ, which he helped to found in Missouri Valley, Iowa.

When my grandparents got married, she was a Presbyterian; they argued about church, and they settled it by going nowhere. Likewise, my dad's mother was a Catholic and my mother was a Protestant. They didn't go to church at all as we were growing up.

Then an unusual thing happened that eventually changed all our lives for the better. A young preacher came to Grandpa Frazier's farm to go squirrel hunting and my Grandpa and he became friends. Years later, when Grandpa died, Grandma had this young man preach his funeral, which was the first time I had ever been in a church. Also, Nora Reel, a friend, began at this time to nag and urge before and after the funeral to get us to come to church. I think we first went there to keep her from coming out and pestering and annoying us more.

All 7 of us were baptized at the same time in the church. After that, we all became active, and those of us remaining still are. My brother, Fillmore, goes to a Church of Christ near Huntsville, Alabama, and my younger brother, Don attends church in Green Bay, Wisconsin.

I am much like my dad was in personality; he never knew a stranger at all. My older brother, Fillmore, was like that too, enjoying people.

When my brother Victor died in 1944, everything changed in my family. Grandpa and Grandma lived on the main farm, the one with the Sears-Roebuck house. We lived on the smaller farm. It was my job to go to the mailbox and bring in the mail. One day in the mail was a telegram; whoever should have delivered it, we later found out, did not have the nerve to deliver it. It read, "We regret to inform you that your son, Victor Kakac, was killed in action in the Battle of St. Lo on August 1, 1944." That was the only notice from the military that we got. When that night's newspaper came out, a story about my brother's death was included because the newspaper knew of the telegram, and many people came to our house to offer their condolences. My mother for the longest while just couldn't believe that it was real, that it had really happened.

My dad had a beautiful tenor voice, and he had sung at countless weddings, funerals, and civic events. He was president of the school board, etc. After Victor died, he never sang again. He even tried to enlist, but the

Army wouldn't take him because of his age. Losing your son is not normal. Your son should lose you.

Victor had been valedictorian of his high school class and went off to the Army the next day after graduation. We had one bedroom at home for us boys, and I had slept in the same bed with Victor until the day he left for the military. On that day, Victor said to me, "In all likelihood, I will never be back," and I couldn't answer him with a word. When he died, I was a freshman in high school. When he was killed the United States Government gave my parents the option of burying him in France in the military cemetery or bringing him back to the United States. They chose to have him buried in France and they never saw his grave. I'm not sure if that was the best decision.

In France, Victor had signed a Gideon's Bible for my birthday present. They took it off his body when he died and sent it to us, along with his bill fold and wristwatch. I felt that this Bible was a message to me.

I couldn't talk about his death to anyone. When I went back to high school, one of my teachers told my class not to ask me about it, that I would talk about it when I felt like I could. Well, I didn't talk about it, and I now know that it would have been better if I had. I didn't want to believe it was true.

Many years later, my sons and I went to Normandy, France, to see where Victor is buried. None of my family had ever been there. There is an organization of women who put flowers on the graves once a year in June. I was impressed by how the cemetery is run by the French people. It is a beautiful, impressive place on the bluffs overlooking the Atlantic Ocean and the famed Omaha beach.

That being said, I think war is a terrible thing and if the politicians and leaders who decided to go to war had to fight the war themselves or fully understood the associated misery and suffering of war, I think there would be much less of it. Still, war may be necessary at times as an absolute last resort. I am a Veteran myself and have many family members including a son who is a veteran.

Chapter 2

SERVING IN THE CHURCHES

To help keep this story straight, I would like to list my churches in time order and the time I spent in each one: Benton City Christian Church, Benton City, MO, 5 years; Novelty Christian, MO, 7 years; Shelbina Christian Church, Shelbina, MO, 7 years; First Christian Church, Fairfield, IL, 34 years; and McLeansboro Christian Church, McLeansboro, IL, 11 years and counting.

I always thought that my best ministry was my first church in Benton City, MO. It was a small church, along a street with a tavern, grocery story, and gas station. I remember alcoholics came often out of the tavern. I always came early to the church to open up. One Sunday, two guys were sitting on the curb outside of the church, saying we were too good for them. Once these two guys got into a fracus with firearms drawn. The sheriff was called, and he said, "You two should put your guns back in your holsters; you're liable to shoot somebody. " I've seen so much in my life.

When I first became a minister and prior to my marriage, there were some people, really good older ladies, who looked after me. Every Lord's day they would have me for dinner, and they were very good cooks. As my friends and family know, I've always loved to eat. These faithful Christians prepared me for the ministry, on-the-job training if you will, in real life ways that Bible college couldn't.

Another man there, the county treasurer, was an elder and just like a father to me. I didn't begin to know the Bible nearly as well as he did. Mr. Pasley, whose son was an engineer who built bridges, was injured in farming accident; he sat on his front porch, reading the Bible.

On Saturday, I would go by this house, and he would say, "Preach a sermon to me," and I would, and he would help me with it. It was like going to college.

In those early days, a newspaper came out of Mexico, MO. The editor would give me a sheet of paper to report weddings and funerals. Right off in this German community I had many young people and weddings. In one wedding, I married a Sydenstricker to a Wilmerskersion and I was Kakac, and the lady I turned in the story to, said she thought I was joking, the names were so crazy.

While I was a student at Lincoln Bible Institute, I preached at a church in Benton City, Missouri, 150 miles away. I drove there every weekend for 5 years. Honestly, I had a hard time finding a church that would take me. When I went on to the next church after Benton City, I wasn't going to resign because I hadn't ever been formally hired in the first place. Before I got to Benton City, two men wanted to be Sunday School Superintendent but got the same number of votes. One of them went to the home of the other and told him to get out of town while his son stood at the side of the house with a shotgun. And he did, because he was afraid of him; his whole family just picked up and left town. The next Sunday, when I arrived on the scene, there was hardly anyone at the church. I had been asked to fill in, but, you know, the church just took off, growing from a few to 130, most of whom were young people. A retired minister there, who had dementia, took me around and introduced me to people, telling me what great people they were and what good friends they were to him, but he couldn't remember their names. It didn't matter, he still really helped me and he was a great friend.

For the youth, we had a group called Christian Endeavor. I remember we used to take roll call by reciting a Bible verse. Most took the easy way out, saying "Jesus wept." I took the lesson directly from the Lookout every week. I spent 5 years there. I still get letters from members of this youth group from time to time, and even attended a reunion for the group several years ago. Those were really good times.

Next I went to Novelty, Missouri, a name that no other city in the United States had. The name came from years ago when an educator moved to that area and started a college. The Novelty of it was that it flourished and was an accredited college until he passed away. At the

Christian Church there, sometimes our attendance would exceed the population of the town, which was 200. Karen Corbin, who attended Central Christian College of the Bible in Moberly, MO, and lived near Atlanta, MO, grew up on a local farm and worked at the bank; she caught my eye and we eventually got married. But more on that later.

In that church was the Perry family, composed of 12 kids. Their dad told them that he would give each of them 160 acres of land, but that they had to live on it. So, there were lots of Perrys in the church. I stayed at that church for 7 years.

In Callao, Missouri, I went to preach a revival. A minister from Memphis, who led the music, had applied for a vacancy at Shelbina, Missouri, but because of his personality and melodrama—like pleading that his children needed shoes—the pulpit committee decided against him but instead approached me and asked me to come there. Our attendance was 350—400 there, and I pastored there for 7 years.

Most of the Christian churches were at one time affiliated with the Disciples of Christ. Over time the organization grew weaker. Much later, about 1965, the organization tried to take the possession of the Christian Church buildings. When this was going on, I said let's invite the representative from the Disciples of Christ to speak and explain, and then let's vote. Well, at the church service on Sunday, the man talked and talked and talked. Finally a woman in the choir stood up and said, 'I make a motion that we keep our preacher and go home to eat dinner.' That, of course, had nothing to do with why the man was there, but he abruptly departed, leaving all his literature there, and we never heard another word from him or his group.

In Shelbina Missouri, I became friends with a black preacher in a black church. All churches were racially segregated at that time. He and I would get together, drink coffee, and talk about the Bible. One of the ladies from the black church called and asked me to be speaker at an occasion to honor the preacher. When I got there, there was a woman sitting on one side of communion table and the minister sitting on the other side. When I started to speak, I talked about what the preacher's wife had to put up with, and the lady in the other chair stood up and said, "I'm not his wife, I'm his sister." That was a bit awkward.

After I finished there was music, etc., and then a woman got up and said, "Now Reverend Kakac will bring the message." I thought I had already preached the message!. The congregations was expecting something a bit longer than my first effort. Brother Hargrove at Lincoln had told us, "Boys, get two sermons and memorize them so that you can give them at the drop of a hat. You'll need them." That's how I was able to immediately preach another sermon. I just didn't pull it out of the air.

The first parsonage I lived in was made for Karen and me from an old telephone office building in Novelty, Missouri. It was the oldest building in town, having been abandoned by the telephone company. The church made two bedrooms, a kitchen, etc., out of it. Prior to that there was no parsonage. Our daughter Kim was born while we lived there.

One of the strangest meals I was invited to was at the home of one of the elders in Novelty. That morning a calf had died, and he told his wife to cook it as a joke. In retrospect, that seems sort of strange, though true nonetheless.

I love American food: meat and potatoes. At my first sermon, I was invited by a president of the bank and his wife to eat at their house. There were several spoons, knives, and forks at every plate. I did not have a clue as to how to use them, and had never experienced multi-course meals. I'm a farm boy from Iowa, and consider myself civilized if I don't use my hands to eat for the entire meal.

In the early days of my ministry, great crowds would attend revivals. It was a time when most people living in a community came into the church.

In Novelty, we had Dr. Condor and his wife across the street from the church. He was a retired veterinarian with an alcohol problem. We were having a revival, and the evangelist, with his approach to people, could sometimes take the bark off a tree. Well, he asked Dr. Condor, who was past 90, to come to church. He did, and eventually wanted to be baptized. The church was full of people, and as Dr. Condor came up out of the water, he said to the people, "I'm going to hoe my row right out to the end." The next day, the evangelist and I went to his home to tell him how happy we were for him. His wife said, "Honestly preacher, I don't know if he can do that or not," and her husband replied, "Well, you haven't read anything in the paper about me recently have you?"

During communion soon after that, Dr. Condor said, "I'm not going to take that! I'm trying to QUIT drinking!" When the offering plate was passed, he dropped his whole wallet in it and said, "You can't beat that, can you now?" At a wedding, Dr. Condor sat right where the bride's mother was to sit, and when the ushers tried to get him to move, he said, "This is my seat, and I'm not moving," and he didn't. He lived many more years and was at church every Sunday.

My wife, Karen, and I met at White Oak Christian Camp in the mid 50's. Our first date was to the church for a revival meeting. We dated about 4 years because I could not afford to get married. I was attracted to Karen's character, good looks, and good family; our backgrounds were very much alike, too. I proposed to her in the church parking lot in Moberly, Missouri.

Another thing that has been very fulfilling for me has been preaching the Ashland revival, near Mill Shoals, IL, every year since 2005. At one time they thought they were going to go out of existence. They even bought a great big stone, putting some of their charter members' names on it, and had it erected to be a monument to where the church used to be.

A few years ago the current minister Braedon Willis said, "Well, I'll come down there and fill in for a while," and that church is running 50 and 60 now. The ministry is a life that even when you are old enough to retire, you don't feel like retiring because of the new people and the enjoyment. I've enjoyed what I've done down through the years. There are some glitches, but where will you not have glitches? I guess I've not found the place where I want to stop yet. Right now I've had the funerals of many people I've married because I've lived so long.

Concerning weddings, funerals, and baptisms, I am always there early. Every wedding, funeral, and baptism is extremely important to my ministry and how I approach evangelism in the community. I get there early because there are always problems that can easily be worked out, but sometimes they just can't be worked out. After all this time, I'm still not sure what to do in cases like that. Sometimes there are just no easy answers and you have to move on.

Especially at funerals, nine times out of ten, there will be last-minute details, such as a song, prayer, family words, and so forth, so I try to be there ahead of time to meet all the people and make sure we are all on the same page. I also have a fear that I'll do something wrong or I won't accomplish what I'm trying to do.

In Fairfield, I had a goal of 52 additions per year. That's about what it takes to make up for the people who move away and people who die. Most years that I was in Fairfield, I was able to real my goal of 52 additions, sometimes even better.

I have so many fears, that I do a lot of praying about every single event, that I'll be able to help the people if they are not Christians, and if they are Christians, it's a great blessing. When I first started my ministry, it was rare that there would ever be a divorce in a family. You had the wedding, a simple wedding, and the two would go off and have a family.

But about 30 years ago, all that changed, and today, 50 percent of marriages go on the rocks, so I try to work ahead of time, through counseling with people. Today, though, it is really hard to get people to come for counseling to think about their coming marriage and its relationship with a Christian life and family. . Consequently, weddings are no longer the joy that they once were because so many people there are not connected with anything that is Christian.

I have this goal to work things out so that the people can get the church in their lives. I remember one of the first weddings I ever had was a young couple in the church, both from good families, good kids; we started the wedding, and a girl had sung a song, and the groom came in and said, "I just can't go through with it. I can't do it."

I told one of the groomsmen to go get his dad, who came and said, "Well, you ARE going to do this." To make a long story short, they got married, they had a great marriage, they have grandchildren today, and their lives have gone along fine. If I had gotten hit cold with that, I don't know what I would have done. I do a lot of praying about things like that to help the church.

One highlight of my ministry happened in Africa in 1976. The Fairfield church had purchased an airplane for a mission in the country of Rhodesia that is now called Zimbabwe. Members of the Fairfield church, Joyce Hastings and Linda Clay and myself, were part of a group of 15 people from different churches that took the trip to Africa. Melvin Spencer, chairman of the missionary committee at Fairfield, paid for my trip. We had built a hospital down there with Dr. Dennis Pruitt, a medical missionary, and Melvin wanted somebody to go down there and see their hospital and their school system.

We flew from here to London, then flew to South Africa, then finally up to Rhodesia. We went out into the bush country where we had this mission that had been in place for years. I was truly amazed; the hospital was amazingly organized and functional. Every day people would come for shots and medicine. There would be hundreds of people sometimes out in front of the hospital. They would build fires and cook meals while they waited for care or visited their loves one who were receiving care.

I went out and preached to those people 4 or 5 times, and others did also. Then we went out and visited the schools, where 12,000 kids were enrolled. They teach them the plan of salvation along with the core subjects: reading, writing, and arithmetic. There were lean-tos and old buildings where they sat on logs that had been split in two. They had kids that were functioning well, and the churches were growing.

As far as selling me on missions, that really did it right there. Shortly after we left Rhodesia, there was a rebellion of people who were not Christians. They took over the country and turned it over to Muslim control. They burned houses and churches. Zimbabwe actually possessed many buildings that were built maybe as far back as King Solomon's time, and they had walls and large buildings that had no mortar. Every stone was made for the weight to go to the center. It was a marvel.

The country still has churches, but the missionaries are no longer there. The hospital is still there, too, still supported by the Christian churches, and still a great mission. There is a great deal of unrest in Africa now, but the churches are still there and functioning. My trip to Africa was an experience that caused me to have a lot of faith in missions.

In all the things that I've done I've really done a lot of praying. There are a lot of things that a minister can't do by himself and never will be able to do himself. I have fears that I won't do the job well enough. I think most people don't think I have a fear in my body, but I do. I've a got this anxiety about not measuring up.

Two incidents have been the saddest times in my ministry.

Mr. Barton of Benton City, Missouri, was not a Christian, but the rest of his family members were baptized believers. But, he promised to be baptized at the next meeting. He passed away before that next week. I worried that I should have tried harder.

At the close of my ministry at Fairfield, I felt too old and not wanted.

As I took the last load out of my office, I cried. It was an emotional experience to leave the office I'd occupied for 34 plus years. Looking back, I realize God had yet another plan for my life - God wasn't finished with me yet.

Chapter 3

HUMOR

Who would think the ministry would be a place for humor? Well, it is, and I have found it in the most unlikely places.

For example, at Benton City, Missouri, we had to start locking the church door due to people coming into the church and messing around. Once you opened the church door you had to walk clear to the front to turn the lights on. This elder had a key to the church, and one of his sons got his key and then hid behind the door and scared me to death when I walked in later. He jumped out and hollered and just on instinct I socked him in the jaw, knocking him down. Well, his dad just never could get over that. I didn't mean to do it, but it just put up a barrier between me and the elder.

The kid soon forgot it and went on to other pranks, but his dad did not. We had an outside bathroom, and the boy would go outside and walk on the board fence around the church property. While I was preaching, here he was trying to walk on that white board fence. Well, he slipped off and came down; he was laying on the ground moaning while I was preaching away.

Another incident happened one time here in Fairfield; Bob Jones, Bob O'Daniel, and others went down to Biloxi, Mississippi to play golf for a week. One Sunday I said in church that I had been reading about this stuff and it looked like as much as they played golf, they'd be really good by now. Bob Jones said he thought the same thing about my preaching.

Anyway, they went down there to play golf, and I found the address of a big Baptist church there, called, and arranged for a church bus to go pick them up on Sunday morning at their hotel. I never told them I had made the arrangements. I guess it was an awkward situation when they got a knock on their door early that Sunday morning by the church bus driver who had come to pick them up for church. They came home and suspicioned something was up, but I never told them I was the one responsible. I had to bite my tongue every time I saw those guys for quite awhile.

In addition, a free will offering during a revival turned out to be a place for humor. When I was asked to conduct a revival in a small church in northeast Missouri, the board asked how much I would charge for the week. I said I guessed $70, which was the amount I was getting paid as minister at Novelty Missouri. They said they didn't know if they could afford that much.

So, I said, well, what about a free will offering, and they said that would be a good idea, but you will need to take up the offering yourself because we have a deacon who steals out of the offering. Anyway, I started taking up my own offering, and after the first two nights, I already had more than the $70 I had asked for, and they knew it.

As a result, they had a board meeting and decided to pay me $70. I laugh now when I think of that, but we did have quite a lot of additions, and the little church grew.

Another funny thing happened in Fairfield. I got to know Big Mary who ran Mary's City Service in Fairfield. One time when I was just about ready to start a funeral, she called me and asked me if I would come down. I asked her if it could be a little bit later, and she said, "No, it has to be right now."

So, I went to her house and she had cats crawling all over me. She really didn't want anything important, but when I got back to the funeral home, I had car hair all over my suit. The funeral director, Chloren Nale, said, "You can't go in there and preach that funeral with all that cat hair all over you. Where have you been?" I told him down at Big Mary's, and he got some kind of a brush and got rid of it all. She loved those cats. When they were crawling all over me, she would say, "They like you, don't they?"

Her grave stone up at Pleasant Grove Christian Church north of Geff has three gas pumps on it: regular, no-lead, and ethyl.

There was a time when couples wrote their own wedding vows. I could never go back to that time period again. Sometimes it's best to just stick to the traditional service. Things become a tradition for a reason.

Another funny thing I had in a church down in Benton City, Missouri. We were having a Vacation Bible School program in front of a packed audience.

There was a kid whose dad I was trying to get interested in coming to church. The dad came to the program, but they didn't get it started when they should have. This man had been drinking, and he stood up and said, "Well, the preacher told me to come down here at 7 o'clock. Now why don't we get started?"

When I left Benton City, Missouri, there wasn't even a filling station there. In the notes of the city council years before, the residents all worked to get the highway built seven miles north of town so that it wouldn't scare the horses. Now that's progressive leadership.

I found out that even Easter can bring some smiles. In Fairfield it was Easter Sunday, and we had a church full of people. During the communion service, the most sacred part of the worship service, I saw this guy come down the aisle dribbling a basketball. I couldn't believe it, thinking well, these young people have gone too far. I thought they were trying to promote something.

He left a note on the communion table and then dribbled out the choir room door. Bob Bruce, one of the deacons, was sitting right there, and I later said, "Bob why didn't you stop him?" Bob said, "I didn't have my whistle, or I would have gotten him for double dribbling."

I called the basketball player the next day; he was a student at the University of Illinois. Somebody had persuaded him that a one-world government should be built in Tokyo and that there should be just one government in the whole world, which he was out promoting. He did the same thing in the Catholic Church and in the Baptist, too. In the Catholic church, some devout lady jerked the basketball out of his hand. It was an excellent steal I am told.

Another interruption was a bird which somehow got into the sanctuary. It was flying all over the place, and I urged people to try to concentrate on the sermon.

The next day I borrowed a BB gun from one of the kids, went down and shot the bird. One of the church ladies said, "Oh, you shouldn't have done that; that is awful bad luck to shoot a bird inside of a church." I had never heard that before.

I used to go to the coffee shop here in town. A Mr. Garman one day said, "You know, the preachers are always saying that they got called to another pulpit somewhere, but it's always to a bigger town and a higher salary. I want to bet you a hundred dollars that you'll leave town before I do." I didn't bet with him, but he's gone and I need to collect the money.

A Holy-Spirit-directed life is based on the question What would Jesus want me to do? One time I got a call to come to Chicago to the First Christian Church because there were a lot of Czech people in the church and they thought because of my Czech name I could do some good.

Sam Miller had a meeting up there, so I went with him to check it out. I went up with Sam, and I noticed there was a great big fence around the building. We parked outside the fence, and when I got back to my car, someone had stolen my battery. Sam said he didn't think I should go to the place where my battery had been stolen.

A city is not my life. Fairfield is the largest town I have ever lived in. I have never had God to audibly speak to me. But I do believe in the guidance of the Holy Spirit and the opportunity to use my talents, and He can do that just the way I am.

One of the most embarrassing times in my life was when I was the state chaplain for Sons of the American Revolution. Ivan Feller and I were on our way to Peoria to stay in a magnificent hotel. My job was to handle the memorial service for all the Sons who had died that year. Ivan said not to worry, as he clued me in on what to say about one particular deceased member.

During the memorial service as I was giving the eulogy for the member who had passed on, a man interrupted me, saying, "He's not dead; he's sitting right over here." I looked over at Ivan and he was smiling.

My mother-in-law had read about the Shelton Gang, and when we decided to move to Fairfield, she said, "What do you want to go to a place like THAT for? The Sheltons live over there! It's nothing but a bunch of gangsters down there!"

The surface of things is often not the way they really are. I suppose there are some ministers who hate their jobs but I always found it a lot of fun. People are more important than plans and programs, and sometimes that's lost in getting the plans and programs in place.

Another incident happened with a couple in Shelbina, Missouri. They were in their 80's, had a wonderful family, and the wife became ill and passed away rather suddenly. He was just devastated.

But not too long later someone knocked at the door of the parsonage, and there he was. He had a phrase that was his byword that he used for everything that came up: "Well, you just as well laugh as cry."

Karen said, "You know the first thing we're going to hear?" I answered, " I suppose you just as well laugh as cry" because that's what he always said. Well, he came in and said that, and Karen got tickled about it. He then said, "What I'm here for is I want to get married."

He and his deceased wife had been a devoted couple, but the truth of the matter is that people who have had a good marriage are the quickest to get married again. I said, "Well, when is this going to be?" and he said, "Just as soon as you can," so I married him.

He was hard of hearing, and the day that he appeared he had gotten kind of excited and had forgotten his hearing aids. He just showed up and wanted to get married. There was no preparation or anything about it.

In a case like that, my neighbor lady had said that if I ever got in a bind, she could come over and be a witness, and I said that my wife would be the other witness. I got down to the place where it said, "You may kiss your bride,' and he couldn't hear what I said for anything. And the bride yelled, "You can kiss me," and my wife and the neighbor lady got to silently laughing until I could feel the floor shaking.

Chapter 4

THE HOLY SPIRIT

What is the Holy Spirit? How does it work in a person? Is it the same thing as a conscience? One of the elders at McLeansboro has asked me the same thing, along with many others over the years.

The Bible tells us that when we become a Christian, it says in Acts 2: 38, "Repent and be baptized everyone of you for the remission of sins and you will receive the gift of the Holy Spirit."

Later on in the Book of Acts, the Holy Spirit is called the Spirit of Jesus, and I believe that a person who has become a Christian and has made that commitment is the same person as before. I don't believe that it necessarily makes you get up and jump over pews or talk in tongues or do strange things at all. But I think that the Spirit of the Lord is with us through everything: our conscience, our intellect, everything, to keep us doing what Jesus would do.

The Bible says the Holy Spirit is The Spirit of Jesus which means that it's blameless or flawless. Of course none of us can be perfect, but there's always that —and I believe it's from God—that determination that you are going to try to do it the way Jesus would have you do it: go where Jesus would go, do what Jesus would have you to do.

And through our prayer life, as we pray every day for guidance and help, I think that the Spirit of Jesus will help us. I know that I have had funerals, I have had weddings, and I have thought, "How can I ever do this, knowing what I know and so forth," and somehow I pray to God, and afterward I've had people come to me and say that I did a wonderful job. God has helped me to do it.

Taking this to our lives, if you are in a room with several doors and wondering which door to take, you're probably going to take the door that's open. If we pray and do the best we can, God's going to open up the door if we follow what is right. We'll go in the right direction.

I believe that the Holy Spirit does things that we do not understand or even realize He's doing it. But I believe that at the time we are baptized we receive the Spirit of the Lord that doesn't leave us and will guide us if we are inclined to pray and inclined to do unto others and to love God with all our heart, mind, and soul. I believe that is the Holy Spirit.

I don't think we have to worry about whether we did the right thing or not. I do not think the Holy Spirit comes and expects strange things out of people. I'm not going to criticize the speaking in tongues. If people feel inclined to get charismatic, then that is their privilege, but generally I think the Holy Spirit is a common sense way of doing what is right when we've made that commitment to try to do what is right.

When the Bible speaks of fruits of the Spirit, that means fruits of the Holy Spirit: love, joy, and peace are the work of the Spirit in our lives. These fruits of the Spirit mentioned in Galatians are not easy things to do, but they are the best way.

In the Book of James, I don't think the Holy Spirit is even mentioned, but the book does say that if we want to endure in this life, we have to do what's right: the Christian way. It was not easy for Paul to write these books while he was in prison, but God directed him to do it. He did it, and we are reaping the benefits today.

Chapter 5

HARMONY IN THE CHURCH

What makes for a harmonious church?

Of course, a lack of sin helps and particularly a lack of selfishness, meaning when a person has to have his own way at the expense of everybody else. When the leaders of the church can be unselfish, not worrying about who is getting the credit for things, there is harmony.

Various places in the Bible address that. It mentions much about the blending of the Jews and the Gentiles. They became harmonious by give and take. Both groups came together IN Christ. They were NEW people. The only way you can get people to realize that they need to be NEW people is to believe that things will work out for the best.

You know, I am not a talented person, and I sure don't mind other people doing things that I can't do, I'm thankful for people who CAN do these things. I have found out in my ministry that there are people who have talent, such as playing the piano or the organ, and then there are people who should just be thankful for those who do possess these gifts. If you have the right spirit, you will be thankful for what others can do.

How does a person working in the church know that he's doing God's will, not his own will? I think God will open a door. God gave a person certain talents that should be used. Those of us who don't have that talent should be thankful for that. I've seen churches split over who is going to be superintendent of the Sunday school. If two people have the same talent, one should step aside graciously.

I have also found that no one can hurt a Christian like another Christian can. This is because the only person that can hurt you is a person that you love. If you love the church and you love what you are doing in the church, and here comes a church member and is the first to criticize, that hurts. The only person that can forgive is the person who has been hurt. You know, maybe the lady next door can't hurt you, but your wife sure can.

Some church people fail to recognize some of the simplest commands of the Lord and examples that the Lord gave us, and they hurt people. I know of people who say things when they know they are going to hurt fellow Christians. I have been hurt more by Christians than by anybody else. How do I get over it? I pray. I just pray about it as hard as I can. And it will happen. Sometimes it will take years.

The kind of love that will break the middle wall or partition down by everyone having a spirit of love for Him is what will make a harmonious church.

Chapter 6

FUNERALS, DEATH, TRAGEDY

My ministry has been highly emotionally charged at times. Funerals, tragedies, and deaths have been times I will never forget.

The first funeral I ever performed was of a farmer whose last name was Baker. His wife was cleaning some overalls with gasoline, and somehow it ignited and burned her to death.

He had a lot of livestock, and in those days farmers took their livestock to St. Louis to sell. In some restaurant down there on 1-70, he met some young woman and married her, bringing her out to his farm. She did not have the same values that he had and she started running around on him. He was just broken hearted about it.

He came to me and asked me to talk to her about it. I went and talked to her, and she broke down, saying she had never been treated that well before. So, she made arrangements with her boyfriend to meet her in a bar in Mexico, Missouri, to tell him she was done with him.

I guess he knew it was coming. He brought a shot gun to the meeting in the bar. When she came in the door, he just blew her head off and then shot himself in the head. I had to preach her funeral, and she had a little boy and little girl by somebody else. Her brothers came up from the Ozark Mountains to the funeral without shirts on, big burly guys, and I did the best I could, not going into details, not mentioning background, doing the best I could to try to bring encouragement to the living.

After the service was over, one of her brothers came to me and, right in front of everybody said, "You did not say one good thing about my sister." I just ignored it, and the undertaker said, "You know, when we go to the cemetery, I'm going to park the hearse right next to the grave, and when you say Amen, get in the hearse and we're going to leave." And that's what we did. I never saw them again. That was a horrible experience for me in my first funeral.

Another tragedy happened on a snowy day in winter time when a soldier and his wife and two or three little kids were coming through town. They hit a section of ice and hit another car head-on. Everyone was killed except the mother and baby.

Somebody called me, and I went out to the wreck. I can still see it all to this day; she was very much alive but paralyzed. Anyway, they got an ambulance and got her out. And there was a baby in the car that was thrown out into a snow bank, and it was not hurt. A nearby farmer picked up the baby and took it into the house. The soldier was from Colorado, and his family later threatened to sue the farmer, saying he should not have moved the baby.

The wife of the driver of the car that the soldier hit was killed, too, and her husband got out of the car and was talking about the accident and fell to the ground dead. I think 7 people died in that accident. That was early in my ministry, and I was called in as a witness.

Believe it or not, there were grave robbers at my grandpa's grave. My grandfather was very close with his money all his life, and my grandmother was about the opposite. After he passed away, she spent a lot. But anyway, when she buried him, she had him buried in a copper casket with a glass door on top.

People used to say about grandpa that when he went, he just wasn't going to go unless he could take his money with him. The family cemetery where he was buried was at the top of a hill, and a patrolman late in the night saw some lights up there. He decided to go up and investigate, and there were a bunch of kids throwing a party up there, and they had grandpa almost dug up. I guess they were inspired by drink and the rumors that grandpa was buried with all his money and they could have got some money from the copper in his casket.

Around that time there was a salesman who had came through the area selling copper grave markers, which shined like a new penny. In no time at all they just turned green. Grandma had bought one of those for Grandpa's casket. When the patrolman discovered them, the kids had already taken that off the casket, and had it loaded in their car.

One Sunday in Libertyville, Missouri, near Farmington, we had church, and everybody had gone, a couple came in, wanting to know if I would hold a funeral for a baby, and I said, yes, I guess I would. I said where will this funeral be? And the man said, "Well, we have the baby out in the backseat of our car. We'd like to have the funeral right now." Obviously now I would never have complied but this was a long time ago and things were just different. Still it was unusual.

We had to drive several miles to a place called Whitewater. It was the custom to dig the grave while the funeral was taking place. They made a pine box and put the baby in there. I was worried, thinking, "How will I talk long enough for them to get this grave dug?" but there was a whole group of men: they knew what they were doing and how to do it.

The next morning the sheriff came to me, asking me if had had a funeral for that baby, and I said, yes, I had. He said, "Well, it's against the law to bury someone in Missouri without embalming." I said that I just didn't know that. The sheriff said that he wasn't going to say anything, but to bear in mind in the future that I couldn't do that again.

I said that they had done that up in the Ozark Mountains for generations, and that's just the way they do it. He said they would probably get somebody else who didn't know the law or care next time.

After that I went to talk to the mother; she had gotten so nervous about the whole thing that her family had taken her to the hospital, so I don't really know how it all turned out. I wasn't accustomed to doing funerals or the laws regarding them, and it nearly got me sick with worry, too.

Another funeral was on a hill. The funeral director said, "Now I'm not going to be there, but my assistant whom I have just hired will be there; he has never had a funeral before, so I would like for you to see him through that funeral."

Two things happened. While I was preaching the funeral sermon, the assistant came and whispered in my ear, "I've got a man passed out. What do I do?" I turned to him and told him that he would have to get him out and get some help. So they took him out under a shade tree, sat him in a chair, and a couple people fanned him until he came back to himself.

The cemetery was on a steep hill. I had purchased a brand new

Chevrolet car and I had very few miles on it. At the gravesite during the committal, I heard a big crash. I looked up and the hearse had rolled over the log they had put under the back wheels and crashed into the back of my new car. The assistant said, "The brakes don't work on that hearse anymore, and I'm really sorry about." It put a big dent in the trunk of my car, and the funeral home fixed it up. Anything can happen at a funeral.

I knew in my early years in the ministry that death is a friend to older people. When a person is suffering and not able to get up and do things and live a meaningful life, death is a friend. It's more like going to sleep for many people. I used to think it was struggling for breath and always a dramatic, extreme experience. But over time I learned to view it much differently.

I would like to tell you about an exciting funeral that I had. It was in Belleville, Illinois, and there was a boy named Jack who had attended church with his mother and dad and his 9 brothers and sisters down in Benton City, MO.

I was in Fairfield at the time, and one day I got a call from Jack's sister wanting to know if I would come to Belleville and do his funeral. He was a young father with 4 children and a wife. He was working for a construction company in Belleville.

I got over to the funeral home and went in to the office to talk to the funeral director who said, "There's a policeman here who wants to talk to you." The policeman said, "Now this funeral is going to be a little different today. We are telling you this because we don't want you to be nervous about anything. There will be 25 highway patrolmen scattered throughout the audience. They will be in uniform, and don't let it bother you; just act like they're not there. If you want to see the family, they are in a room, and we've got a person stationed at the door so that no one can go in."

I went in to the family which was all heart-broken, but I still didn't know what was going on. The policeman said, "When you are finished with the funeral, there will be policemen outside the door leading the way to the hearse. And when we get to the cemetery, there will be other policemen, and whenever you have said your final thing, just get in your car and leave. My son, Kevin, had gone with me as a driver. I told him about it, and he said they told him where to park the car.

To this day, I'm not sure exactly what that was all about. The family never talked about it. Someone mentioned something about a construction accident associated with violent emotions and threats from the affected parties. Clearly the authorities thought it warranted to take extreme precautions.

Another thing I did—and everyday is an exciting thing—I had a young man in the congregation, one of 5 brothers, big tall, strong-looking good people. This young man worked for a funeral home which had built a brand new, still unused funeral home. The owner told this young man, "If you want to get married there, you can use the funeral chapel for your wedding. I'll let you use all the funeral cars."

It seemed like a good idea; it had never been used for a funeral. I thought that was nice. The church where the bride went was being renovated. The groom's mother sang for every wedding and funeral there was in the community. She came in to me one day, really angry, saying, "Are you going to let them have their wedding in a funeral home? You were for it, and they want to do it, and they have asked me to sing. I'm not going to do it. I've sung all those songs about "going down the valley one by one."

It caused a big commotion in the family. After that was over, I thought I would never do something like that again as long as I lived. Yes, no more weddings in funeral homes for me. I learned my lesson on that one. The couple today is happily married. The husband is a football coach in a college in Colorado. Everyday as a minister you run into things you never dreamed would be possible. It's not what a lot of people think the ministry is like. There's absolutely nothing dull about it.

Many people have asked me where a person's spirit goes when he dies. When a person dies, he goes directly to Paradise with the Lord if he is a Christian. And a person who has turned down Christ goes directly to Hades.

And then there is a final Judgment, a final separation when people go to either Heaven or Hell. It's kind of like in a court of law. If somebody steals some chickens, a person is a free man until the judge says it's the penitentiary for him. There will be a new Heaven and a new Earth.

In a moment, in the twinkling of an eye, First Corinthians 15 tells us that we will be changed. We'll have a body that lasts forever. I think we will know each other. If I knew how He is going to do all this, I would be

God, but I don't know all of that, but I believe it because of all the other things that have come true that He has promised.

I have had hundreds of calls in the middle of the night.

I received a call from the sheriff in Shelbina at 2:00 a.m. One of the ladies in the church had 1 son, always a problem, who gathered brush at the base of a tree, poured gas on it, crawled up in the tree, tied a rope to a limb, threw a lit cigarette into the brush, and then jumped with the noose around his neck.

The sheriff wanted me to go tell his mother. I called a close friend of hers and we went to tell her. She, of course, knew something was awfully wrong when she saw us two in the middle of the night.

Another time, late one night, I was called to the hospital. A young mother was delivering triplets and two of the babies did not live. I was there to offer comfort and prayers for the parents and grandparents. It was a very sad situation. However, the surviving triplet is a happy, healthy teenager today, and his parents and grandparents are greatly blessed by his life.

Chapter 7

FEELING GOD'S PRESENCE

God is present everywhere every minute of every day. However, I have had times when I felt His presence particularly and I felt His peace.

The way the communion service in our church was conducted—including the music and the elders' discussion of the scriptures—was when I especially felt God's presence. If I were having a difficult time preparing myself to deliver the sermon, the communion service usually really helped. Church music is supposed to present to individuals a message from God; that's what all my favorite hymns do.

Another time I strongly felt the presence of God was when Wayne Smith was in Fairfield for a revival meeting, and we had fifteen people decide to be Christians. Wayne was the minister of a large church in Lexington, Kentucky, and he said it had been a long time since he had had that many people come forward at the same time. Our church was really growing at that time. Our church really experienced the presence of God during that time.

At Shelbina, Missouri, we had a Christmas Eve program. During one of these, a lady came to me, saying her daughter wanted to be baptized. This girl later became Miss Missouri. Four other girls came forward with her. We had a communion service and a baptismal service. I felt that was a time when the Lord was really with us.

Another very special time was my first baptism. We had twins, the Barker sisters, who went into the baptistry at the same time and were baptized together. That was another time I really felt the Lord was there. Actually, if you read the Psalms, you read about services and you read about praising. I think we miss the presence of God in some of our elaborate services today with all the entertainment.

Peace, perfect peace. Lots of time when things would get confusing, I would go to the sanctuary and sit there for a while. That is what really helped me to find peace through prayer. When a person is baptized, I felt a sense of peace. Today when you listen to the news, it's all so negative and frustrating that you need times of peace like that. Going fishing for a few hours, I thought about things I could change and I could look at all of God's creation and see how wonderful it all was—that was the easiest way for me to experience peace.

All sins are equal in weight in God's eyes. We all know that the consequences of sin on this earth are severe. But as far as what separates us from God, sin is sin; it can be anything. For example, David committed murder and adultery and was forgiven. The amazing part of the amazing grace is that I believe there are going to be a lot more people in Heaven than many Christians feel there will be. I believe that God truly forgives if we ask to be forgiven. And the Book of Revelation teaches that no man can count the numbers of people. We can feel God's presence and His peace when we are forgiven.

Chapter 8

Excitement of Christian Ministry

Ministers are few and far between now. I'd like to explain to would-be ministers how the Christian ministry is an exciting life.

Christian ministry is a worthwhile thing to do even though it has somehow become not the "in" thing to do with a lot of people. When I was in college, they taught us as best they could on how to be a minister. It's been an exciting thing ever since.

Our teachers told us that the minister should plan to use the morning for study, for sermons and lessons, weddings, funerals. In the afternoon we were told to do our calling. If you live where there is a hospital or a nursing home, learn who the people are to visit and when to make the rounds.

But, I soon found out that the ministry is much more exciting than that. Lots of times I would go down to the office and maybe I would be there ten minutes or a couple of hours, and then someone would call and say so and so was taken to the hospital in Evansville and you need to go see her. When someone tells you to do that, you go immediately! There's hardly any way a preacher can refuse to do it.

So, you get in your car and you go over there and do the best you can. If you have studies that you need to do, you might have to leave out the nursing home and the hospital visits.

When I first came to Fairfield, our hospital would be full every day and there would be people even out in the hall with curtains around them. You could spend a lot of time there; of course, now they don't have that many patients.

No matter what happens, though, Sunday keeps coming whether you're ready or not. You don't have any trouble at all when you're in the full-time ministry trying to find something to do. It's never a dull moment.

I used to love to come to the office every morning because every day would be different. The advice we got in college of using mornings and afternoons hardly ever worked out that way in any week of my ministry.

Before my time, ministers were paid with chickens and roasting ears. And on that theme, Mrs. Downer, the wife of our church janitor, called me one day saying that someone had advertised in the Wayne County Press that they had a sweet corn patch which people could come to and pick corn for free.

She wanted me to go and pick her some sweet corn and bring it up to the high rise where they lived. I didn't have time for picking sweet corn, so I went to the grocery story and got four ears for a dollar wrapped in cellophane. I took it up there and gave it to her, and she said, "Oh, you didn't need to wrap it up so pretty."

Sometimes you are in the car thinking about what you are going to say instead of sitting in the church office and doing it.

The ministry today needs people who like to work with people and are dedicated to the cause of Christ.

Even with funerals and weddings, each one is completely different from all the others.

Here is a list of things I advise a young preacher to do and not to do.

Be real. Do not act like someone you are not. Do not adopt the "holier than thou" attitude.

Do not have favorites. Do not have special friends.

Dress neatly. Stay away from fads.

Have your own time for prayer and Bible reading.

Do what you tell the people to do.

Pay your debts around town.

Do not spread rumors.

Be confidential. There are things that you will need to take to the grave, including many things which would have been interesting in this book.

Don't gossip, spend too much money, dress slovenly, fail to prepare sermons, or fail to be available.

Don't argue scripture and don't beat people over the head with a Bible.

I would also like to pass along to young ministers what I've learned about scripture:

Every time I read the Bible I learn something I did not know before.

The same is true in preaching from scripture that I have used many times.

Living a life in accordance to the scriptures is a powerful thing. The Bible truths expand over time.

The Bible gives us the Way, The Truth, and the Life.

God will speak to you if you go to his word with a receptive soul.

I've learned a lot about human nature, too:

There are two sides to every board. This includes marital fights, etc.

People will respond in kind to your attitude. If you are glad someone is going to hell, they will become angry with the truth. If you tell them, with love in your heart, they will take the truth. If you don't have love, don't preach it.

Everyone expects the preacher to be good. There is no value in trying to get as close to the world as you can.

There is good in anyone who has a mother.

The best are not perfect. Follow Jesus instead of trying to be perfect.

What I've learned about death:

It is like birth. We all experience it. I do not fear death. It can be a friend to those who suffer.

In the experience of death, you will be glad for the good you have done.

I have never met a person, on their death bed, who has been sorry they have been a Christian.

Be ready for death. It is never the one that you think that will go first.

What I've learned about preachers:

Too many are jealous of other preachers.

Too many are seeking a bigger and better position.

Too many are fighting something: fault, sin, etc.

They become more tolerant as the years go by.

What I've learned about addiction:

Addictions can be broken. But sometimes it takes a lot of previous failures and effort, including intense prayer to finally overcome.

Addictions are symptoms.

You replace addiction with positive things in your life.

Here is what I've learned about money:

Do not spend more than you have.

Figure ahead of time how much you can afford and when you do spend it will be less stressful.

Work out a budget

When you are older, don't borrow.

Money will not make you happy. Only the right use of money can make you happy. Even more importantly, poor money decisions can cause misery.

I've dealt a great deal with husbands and wives; here is what I have learned about them:

What it takes to separate is far more severe than what it takes to stay together.

Take consideration for the days the other half doesn't feel good. Help them feel good.

Never run down your spouse in public.

Being married will keep you from being an old maid or bachelor.

Marriage is God's way of making your life complete.

When I see two people going down the street holding hands, I'm not surprised at a divorce.

What I've learned about politics and government:

Politics is not the answer. Christian politicians are what we need.

The world isn't saved by politics, and preachers should stay out of it.

Create a Christian society with Christian leaders and they will do the right thing—no matter their exact political persuasion, be it Republican or Democrat.

We need a lot more true Christians in government.

What I've learned about myself:

I have few talents. So, I have to rely on talented people in the ministry. I've found that talented people are willing to help.

Music is where I really have to ask for help.

I can't ACT profound, or highly educated, like a amazing orator or like a better person than others. I am most effective when I just am myself.

I can never tell when I have done the most good or bad. Sermons that I am not happy about help others.

Sometimes when I think I have a winner, it flops.

What I've learned about special meetings:

People are not looking for a big church. They are looking for a place to serve.

A Sunday School class is the perfect "small group."

People can find better entertainment on TV. Stick to the message for long-time goals.

What I've learned about marriage:

One must "bring to" not "take from" a marriage.

Children do not want to live with one parent or the other. They want to live with both parents.

What I've learned about happiness and joy:

Joy and happiness come from within and have not much to do with material things.

Happiness has a lot to do with what is in your heart. When I was happiest was when all the kids were home and I was broke.

What I've learned about getting along with people:

The way you treat people will eventually come back to you.

People will react differently on various days.

People that butter you up will stab you in the back.

When one comes in for a conversation, look at the last thing he says before leaving.

People will generally do what you expect them to do.

When it comes to working with people, depend a lot upon God.

What I've learned from my grandchildren:

Don't brag. They are like too many other kids.

They will make you proud.

They will really love you.

They are so much like their dads and moms were.

What is the most vital ingredient in becoming a successful minister:

Staying power. I have married, buried, and baptized mothers and dads, sons and daughters, and grandchildren in the same family.

What does the world need most:

God, Christ, the Church.

Ministers who will minister instead of entertain.

Chapter 9

CHANGES IN THE CHURCH AND CULTURE

I have lived through much change in the church and in our culture. The Church has leaned too far towards the entertainment. Instead of trying to bring the Bible message to people and trying to help them live, churches have attempted to compete with secular activities such as popular music and movies. This has all taken place in my lifetime, and the church has decreased instead of increased. Perhaps the church should be presenting itself as a counter-cultural alternative rather than a modern lifestyle.

When I was kid, church people helped widows and orphans. We had a lady in our neighborhood whose husband hurt himself with a circular saw, got lockjaw and died. All the time I was growing up, neighbors made sure she had wood for the winter, canned goods, and took care of her. I don't see that happening as much anymore. This has been a drastic change. We can't rely only upon governmental assistance to help those in need. Churches probably can deliver aid to those who need it in a more efficient fashion, if we would just do it.

When I first started preaching, you could put a sign on a telephone pole about a revival, and everybody would come. Parents wanted their kids to know the Ten Commandments and the Sermon on the Mount, but now they don't. I feel this is at least related to the introduction of the television into our homes. Before television, there was nothing else for kids (or parents, for that matter) to do, so they came to church. That's where young people came to meet their mates. Our culture has changed until the church is not as important. But, I think the way our culture is going, revivals and a larger influence of the church will be return. People are beginning to see the need of a standard of some kind. I think I see a general realization that the predominant secular norms of today are not meeting our needs.

If revivals make a comeback, there are not enough evangelists to fill the pulpits. When I graduated from Lincoln Christian College in 1955, there were over 60 future preachers in my class. Last year there were 5. There is a huge shortage. I talked to a preacher in Louisville, Kentucky, who said that many the ministers in this church of several thousand are former school teachers who have transitioned mid-career to the ministry. There is nothing wrong with that but we need more traditionally educated ministers as well.

The most joyful time of the church when I started preaching in 1952 was when a person accepted Christ and was baptized and the change that was taking place in that person's life. That was what church was all about 64 years ago. The churches would have revivals when many people came forward, and the people would talk about what happened each night and how it was going to make a change, and the churches really grew.

The exciting part of a church 64 years ago was a person accepting Christ. I feel like there is not so much excitement anymore because the exciting part of the church today is the entertainment. And while we have some fine entertainers and fine music, you can get that on TV or radio.

The excitement of going to church is expressed as, "Now wasn't that a wonderful program? Wasn't that a wonderful play? Wasn't that a wonderful sermon?" But you hardly see anybody baptized any more. The greatest joys I used to have as a minister was seeing someone become a Christian.

And sometimes in a community where someone's lived an ungodly life and maybe the rest of the family is connected to the church, here this guy would come and finally decide to become a Christian. That was talked about and considered a great victory.

Today because a lot of our big mega churches are televised, they are trying to do away with the communion and the beautiful music that goes along with that because it doesn't fit in with the time schedule. And they do away with the invitation where people come and give their lives to the Lord because that doesn't fit into the time schedule either.

So you have an entirely different reason for having joy in the church than we had 64 years ago in the church. When I first started preaching, I didn't know as much as the elders did; I hadn't been a Christian for very long. I remember this little church where I started; we had 25 baptisms in one meeting. I was going to school at the same time. I came home at Easter time and we had this revival and these many conversions took place. That was the main topic in the community. It just isn't that way anymore.

I think the things in church that truly bring us joy are absent. People are the same today as they were 2,000 years ago; the same things that make people upset today, made people upset 2,000 years ago.

The ministry is probably more difficult today than it was when I started preaching. When I started preaching, even parents who had nothing to do with the church wanted their children to go to youth groups so they'd learn right from wrong. It's not like that anymore.

The morals of our country have slipped tremendously in the last 30 years. Education has improved, financial knowledge has improved, and science has advanced, but I don't think the church has kept up with it. I think the church has tried to become like the world. Back when I started, people wanted to hear the gospel, and now people want the church to be consumer- friendly.

It's so difficult for us to be Christ-like because of our culture. There have been cultures—I read the Bible through every year—and every time I read the Old Testament, those people turn away from God and go into captivity and all kinds of terrible things happen to them; then they cry out to God and He brings them back and restores them—it seems like when we develop the culture when we believe that WE are doing it instead of God doing it, we slip back every time.

It's necessary, but very difficult, for a person to become a Christian and remain faithful. You have to pay attention to it daily, pray daily, and keep in contact daily.

When I first started preaching, I could go to somebody's house, and the people would be so glad to see me, they'd invite me in and talk to me. Then when television came in, and I was breaking up somebody's TV program, they didn't want to see you anymore. They still don't. They don't want you to come and interrupt.

Now churches are reaching out to addicts and I'm really glad about that. What it takes to help an addict helps others because we are all addicts, to sin or something. I guess the same things that keep you an alcoholic keep you in a lot of different sins. God is the only one who can help us, and He can and will.

I think Christian churches are trying to attack these addiction problems. It's actually really needed. When help is done from the angle that it's the Lord doing the helping, these programs can be successful. When people with problems go to church and find the emphasis is on entertainment, they don't come back because that's not what they are looking for.

People drift into church and then drift out of church because they are wanting to be recognized, to be served rather than to serve other people. They come to church for what they can get out of it, not for what they can give to it. I read a story about a man down in Kentucky who wanted to have engraved on his tombstone, "He hoped in the Lord," but the engraver made a mistake and put, "He hopped in the Lord." This may illustrate the drifting, inconstant nature of many of us Christians: we hop in, and then out of the Lord.

Chapter 10

BAPTISMS

One of my very first baptisms was when I was holding a revival down in Libertyville, MO, out in the country; this was the oldest Christian Church west of the Mississippi. Today it's a museum owned by the historical society. At the front of the church, there were two doors: one for the women and one for the men, plus a balcony for the slaves.

They didn't believe in baptizing people in the church; it had to be done in running water. During the first revival I had down there, I dug an area out in the river bed because, after church, we were to have a baptism. One of the elders who was coming down to the river with me had a spade, and I told him that I had already dug it out, and of course where I had dug the night before was all filled in with sand. You had to dig out an area right before the baptism, and you had to baptize upstream instead of downstream, because if you baptized downstream, their feet would come right up to the surface. The elder had to teach me how to baptize a person in running water.

Whenever I started preaching, baptisms were so important; everybody in the congregation was filled with gladness. It seems today many do not want to be baptized in front of people. Baptisms are a teaching tool. They should be happy occasions that people are willing to wait for.

Another situation that has come up a few times has been with people who are full grown and decide they want to be baptized again, feeling that when they were young and baptized they didn't know what they were doing or thinking they were only baptized because everybody else was doing it.

What I try to do in a case like that is to explain that nobody knows everything there is to know about Christianity at the end of life, let alone when you are a babe in Christ. There's a lot to learn.

At the outset you know that you are a believer and that you want to do something about it, but the Christian life is one of growth. The people whom I have baptized again have all been godly people.

I don't know that I ever knew a better man than Herschel Berg, and he came to me and asked me to baptize him again because, even though he was about 90, he was troubled that he had been baptized when he was young and didn't have a firm understanding of what he was doing. I did it, and he had peace of mind about it afterwards. I'm not sure it was necessary but it was a good thing and I was glad to be a part of it.

Chapter 11

SERMON METHOD

As a minister, I eventually developed a method for writing a sermon, through trial and error, of course. It's not a fool-proof way to compose a sermon, but it has worked well for me.

To begin with, I do not go on too long. I learned this important lesson in seminary and I still go by it.

I plan by asking who, what, where, and why does it make a difference?

I also learned in class to not make personal remarks to any individual. It is necessary to preach to the whole congregation because my speech teacher said it was unethical to say something personal when that person can't answer you back.

I use commentaries, and I read the Bible a lot. I went to college and took classes on sermon preparation but have learned much more through experience.

Generally, I don't re-use prior sermons. Many people have asked me why I don't just start recycling old sermons that I have already created. The answer is that I generally enjoy the process of sermon creation and get a great deal from the process personally and spiritually.

At one point I had kept all of my previous sermons for literally decades. Several years ago during a period of time I was going through it seemed like the right thing to do to throw them all away. I didn't figure anyone would ever read them anyway. In retrospect, I'm not sure if that was a good decision or not.

Chapter 12

THE RESTORATION CHURCH

Our brotherhood is a result of the Restoration Movement which originated in Kentucky in the early 1800's. Its purpose was to return the church to the principles of the primitive church of the New Testament.

I don't believe that the church in this world will ever be completely restored because the congregations differ from each other so much. It's an on-going thing to try to make the church what it should be, based upon a particular denominational interpretation.

Probably the main thing that the Restoration Movement focused upon and the thing that we receive the most credit for is the restoration of the weekly communion service. Acts 20 says the early church met on the first day of the week for that purpose. They were to remember that we have a Savior, and they observed the communion service.

The Restoration Movement has tried to restore the one church, but it now has three divisions in it: The Church of Christ which does not believe in music instruments in the service, the Christian Church, and the Disciples of Christ.

One of the main reasons pioneer churches didn't have music was the scarcity of instruments which were principally made at that time in Europe. When churches started having pianos, the defense of "We've never had that before" was used and the instruments were rejected. Further pianos were associated with saloons. I feel I am a brother to another Christian, whether he wants an instrument or not.

The biggest reason the church has not won the world to Christ is that the church is not willing to pay the price. The church has adjusted to the world. Standards have deteriorated in the church just as they have in society.

It used to be that the church stood for the right, no matter what, and now we talk in terms of being people-friendly rather than standing for the things that are right according to the Bible.

What is it that makes people want to come to church and to become Christians? I think that within every person there is a strong desire to do what God wants us to do. A lawyer in the church at Shelbina said, "Preachers have one thing in their favor, and that is people want to get right with God no matter how far away from God that they might be. Most people come to church to learn about God and His plan of salvation. They want to hear it preached at the services."

In some communities, people no longer see anything that they want to aspire towards in the church. They don't see the church as offering that salvation. Signs and programs won't do it. When I came to Fairfield, anywhere I would go people would say, "You have some strong Christian families in the church," and they admired that and they talked about it. Churches need to create a Christian culture within a community that people admire and want to be a part of.

Chapter 13

COUNSELING SITUATIONS

Counseling has always been a place where angels and ministers fear to tread.

That makes me think of a lady in Mcleansboro, who decided she wanted to be baptized. She said, "I have this fear of water, and you're going to have to get me over this fear before I can do it."

Once while at a party on a lake people threw her overboard, not knowing she couldn't swim. That boat went on, and another boat came along, saw her floundering, and picked her up and took her to the bank. Now she said she cannot even get in the shower without having panic attacks. But, she said, she wanted to be baptized.

I advised her that before we did the baptism, she should go to the doctor and talk about her severe anxiety and explain the situation to him. Her doctor told her to just say a little prayer and then go ahead and do it, that the Lord would be with her. She came to me and said, "That's what I'm going to do."

However, our baptistry has steps in it and is so small you can barely baptize a child in it, so I said, "Let's go up to Fairfield; they have a large baptistry there, with a hand railing."

Actually, to baptize a person is an easy thing because you don't lift any weight. The person rises to the surface. So that's what we did. I baptized her and it went off like clockwork. There was no panic, nothing. I prayed a lot beforehand, and when it was all over, they were just as happy as could be when she came up out of the water.

Another case that took counseling took place in my first church. The

Presbyterian church closed in that town. From that church an elderly gentleman wanted to come to our church but he didn't think I was strong enough to baptize him. He didn't realize that it was not a matter of strength to do that. So, he made me go down into the basement of the church and do a chin up to see if I was strong enough to do the job. I did it on a pipe down there, a heating pipe, and proved to him that I had the strength to do it.

Then, I had a girl to come for counseling once a week for about two months. She was afraid she was going to die. She was a high school girl. I told her to go to her minister, and she didn't want to do that.

I had met her at Oil Belt Camp. I told her that kids who want to be baptized will be afraid to go to sleep at night for fear that they won't wake up and can't be baptized. I asked her if it were something like that, and she said yes it was.

I said, "Are you a Christian?" and she said, "No, I'm not." I had prayer with her and told her, "You go down to your preacher and tell him you want to become a Christian. I think that fear will leave you and you will be better." It worked. I saw her a couple years later, and she said she was cured.

You have a lot of things like this in the ministry that people don't realize you deal with on a daily basis. There is so much of it that is a gray area of what to do. You just do the best you can. That's what I've always tried to do and go from there. Some of these things, looking back on them, seem humorous, but at the time they happened they were serious problems.

Chapter 14

WHY ALL MY CHURCHES HAVE GROWN

I've been thinking about all the churches and, not because of me, they have all grown, not just in number, but spiritually which is the most important. I have tried to think of what made them grow. Actually, every church that I have been called to by the Lord, the door has been opened to me in a surprising fashion. In each, right before I got there, they had had some kind of a serious problem on their hands.

This is the main reason they grew: the church came first in my life. It came before my family, and they knew it. I feel that doing the Lord's work made me a better father. There were many ball games I didn't get to go to because I had a wedding or a visitation, but the kids understood that was part of my job, and I think that made them realize how valuable the church is. I don't think it hurt a thing that I put the church first. God wanted me to do that with my life, and it indirectly made me a better dad.

Another reason the churches grew was that I did not turn down weddings or funerals for any personal reason. Many of the contacts I have made for the church and for people coming into the church, were people I had ministered to through weddings and funerals, and I had no other way of reaching those people. I took those weddings and funerals, even though I missed a lot of things with my family.

This spilled over into vacations, too. In Missouri, we had the car loaded and were ready to leave when I learned that one of the oldest and most faithful members of the church had just died; I was the only preacher in the community, so I stayed home and did my job. It was a soul-searching experience, but I did it.

Another reason for church growth was that before my own personal comfort I served the church. If you wait until you feel like doing something, it's not going to get done. For example, one day I was scheduled to have a wedding, and I had a 102 fever. I had actually called the youth minister and asked him to do it; I felt that bad. The youth minister couldn't do it for some reason, so I went ahead and officiated at the wedding. In all these things, it wasn't so much what I did; it was that I tried to put the church first in what I did. And the churches, every single one, grew.

Another reason the churches grew was that I took part in all of the community events I was asked to. That meant prayers, speaking at the Lions Club, etc. Through those experiences I met people and was able to influence them to come to church. I found out early in my ministry that you don't force people to come to church. You don't pressure them to come to church. But if you become their friend and are genuinely interested in their lives, many times they will decide to come to church.

In addition, my giving was a factor. I tithed from what I earned and from what was given to me. I had a huge debt with my son Kevin's hospitalization during most of the first two years of his life at Children's Hospital in St. Louis, but I kept tithing. Somehow the Lord blessed us and we came out of it. I wanted to give as the scriptures say that I should be giving.

It's very important to visit people in the hospital or in the nursing home. I did that nearly every single day. I don't have oratorical or musical talent that many ministers do, but I do what I can in other ways.

Next, I showed no favoritism in the community. Democrat, Republican, Lions, Rotary, rich, poor, or in between. I showed no favoritism at all. In that way I met new people.

Finally, I did not take part in any church conflict. For example, at my second church, the former minister had some moral problems, he resigned, and the church hired me to replace him. He had, however, talked to some of the members about getting his life back in shape and returning in a year. A controversy arose about whether he should be allowed to do that.

I told the church that I wanted no part of that argument, that they could let me knew if they wanted me to come back or if they didn't want me to come back. At the church in Shelbina, they were voting on whether to be a Christian Church or a Disciples of Christ Church. I never mentioned either group from the pulpit, never once. I just preached the gospel.

I just feel that the principles I have just given are the reasons the churches have grown. I learned these things when I was in Bible college. Each week we had some wise people come in for "The Clinic." These successful people would discuss with us various problems that could come into the church.

They all said. "Let the church handle its own problems. Just stick with the gospel; that's what you are called to do. Preach the Bible, preach sermons, and stay out of those things that divide people.

While all the churches grew, I don't deserve any of the credit. It's just what anybody with common sense would have done. I have been thinking of what has made up my ministry, and that's the work ethic I followed.

At McLeansboro, I told them that I had one requirement: that I not attend board meetings, that they could run their own affairs, and that I would just preach the gospel in the small church that averages about 30 people.

Chapter 15

WEDDINGS

I have done hundreds and hundreds of weddings during my ministry, and unusual things can happen during them. Here are some that come to mind.

I performed a wedding at the Bethel Church, which was in an old German community. The sanctuary had a wooden floor and a platform about 5 feet up from the floor. You couldn't begin to step up on it, you had to take the stairs on the side.

The wedding was up on the platform, and the best man during the ring exchange portion dropped the ring, which plinked off the platform and rolled two or three pews back. He just vaulted off the platform, crashed to the floor, crawled under the pews, got the ring back, then rolled and hopped back onto the front of the platform. The crowd was in stitches.

Another time when I was in Shelbina, there was a girl and boy, who decided they wanted to be married in the hospital just before she delivered the baby.

I drove to Hannibal, Missouri, about 40-50 miles away, to the hospital and tried to explain that perhaps it would be better to wait until after the baby was born and get married in the church. The mother of the bride did not appreciate my logical approach, got upset and swore at me with great talent.

Another large wedding was planned for a girl, extensive arrangements had been made, including reserving 300 plates at the local Elks club. A pianist and a photographer were engaged, and the church was full of people, but the bride and groom never showed up.

It came time for the wedding, and I was just wringing my hands. I didn't know what to do. The music was playing, the photographer was poised. The groom's dad was a highway patrolman who lived at Grayville. I got him on the phone, and he said, "Oh, didn't they tell you, they went away and got married."

So I called the Elks and told them no one would be eating there, and they said, "You better be wrong. We've got food up here for 300 people." Then I had to go out and announce to the church full of people that there was not going to be a wedding.

I did all these weddings at no charge. If they gave me something, I accepted it, but if I thought they couldn't afford it, I gave it back as a gift.

All of the wedding and funerals I prayed about a great deal, feeling they were a very important part of my ministry. I always tried to be there early to make sure things went alright. I found out, too, that just because a great deal of money is spent on a wedding doesn't necessarily make the service more meaningful or beautiful, or the marriage more likely to last.

I was asked by a young girl, obviously pregnant, to perform a wedding for her and her boyfriend. She was attending a rock concert at a local church at the time and said she just had a few minutes to do it as there was a musical group performing that she didn't want to miss. They wanted to get married between acts and just get it over with! I told her that I couldn't do that.

The preacher at the Westside church in Springfield, IL, which is the largest church in the state, had a sister who belonged to the church in Shelbina. Her husband passed away. She was a widow and there was a real nice fellow in the congregation she got together with. They were going to have a wedding, but none of her 7 children were in favor of it.

She was a good person, and he was a good person. They came and talked to me, and we made arrangements to have the wedding right there in the living room of the parsonage.

But, the day that they got married, the kids and the grandkids all decided that they would accept it and get over it, and my living room wouldn't begin to hold all the people who came. We had to move it over to the church. It all worked out. He was good to her, and he was good to her children and grandchildren.

Chapter 16

TRANSIENTS

Another ministry of the church, and of the minister, is to help people in need. Because the Fairfield church was on a well-traveled north-south highway, we had many people over the years stop in the church and ask for money.

Transients and needy people are a part of a minister's job, too. A lady in the church at Fairfield told me, "You help those people, and I'll keep that fund up," and she did.

Once a young mother came in needing money for diapers; she had cigarettes in one shirt pocket and a cell phone in the other. I gave her ten dollars for diapers, and right after that I was in Huck's convenience store, and she was in there buying lottery tickets.

All the transients have told me, "I'll pay the church back," and all but one have not. The one who did was from Kansas. His car broke down, we paid to get him going again, and he returned the money.

One homeless person came in wanting a place to stay. I sent him out to the Crown Motel, and he returned, complaining, "I'm not staying in that room; it's not even air conditioned."

Once a man came in off the highway and said, "I don't want any money. I just want you to write a letter to my family, here's the name and address, and tell them how much I've cleaned up my life. I'll be forever grateful." He didn't refuse the ten dollars I offered him, and later as I drove past the liquor store, I saw him going in there.

For at least 10 years, two homeless men came in separately about twice a year, in the spring and fall. Hacker and Rhodes always stopped by the church to see me and get a handout. Once I was in St. Louis and saw Hacker hitchhiking along the interstate. I picked him up and brought him back to Fairfield. Once I asked Rhodes why he chose to live like that, and he said, "It used to be a lot of fun."

Across the road from the church to the east for years was a filling station. I saw a man there for many hours with a cardboard sign. It got on my conscience after a while, so I said, "Can I buy your dinner for you?" to which he answered, "Oh, no, I've done really well this morning."

The bottom line though is that I have felt very fortunate to be in a position through the church to help people at times of extreme need in their lives. I never really thought it was my job to try to screen out the "scammers" from the people who "really needed help." I figure if you are in my church asking for help, you really do need some sort of help. And I stopped being disappointed if I saw them using the money we gave in a less than ideal way. I just hoped that I might be a small part of eventually getting these people back on their feet, even if we didn't get them all the way there while they were in my little town.

Chapter 17

TIMES REQUIRING MUCH PRAYER AND PATIENCE

All funerals take much thought. What you say can be very important. I try to prepare myself by asking what I think the deceased and their family would like to leave as their legacy, and to try to briefly capture the essence of the deceased person's life. For weddings, I try to make them as meaningful as possible by talking to the bride and groom at length and really getting a feel for what they are trying to accomplish in the service and the themes they wish for me to focus on to make their service special and meaningful.

For baptisms, I stress most of all that sins are forgiven. I have talked to almost of all of them beforehand and make sure they grasp the significance of what they are doing and the context of what this crucial step means in a Christian life.

In marriage counseling, I try not to take sides. I just try to improve communication between the two people and perhaps try to summarize the progress we are making and occasionally reframe nagging arguments and concerns in a more constructive way. I never wish for the couple to think that I am going to be able to give them an easy quick solution to their issues.

In a funeral, you don't have to worry about the person who cries; it's the person who can't that has problems.

A physician friend of mine Dr. Pruitt and I visited a former soldier in a hospital. He had been an honor award winner for his service to his country, but had become a very troubled person. He sat staring straight ahead for long periods of silence. Dr. Pruitt was quite familiar with what we now call post traumatic stress disorder (PTSD) and the persistent social and emotional problems these soldiers can experience. These problems can be overcome with great faith and persistence and perhaps most importantly, professional help.

Chapter 18

EXCUSES FOR NOT GOING TO CHURCH

1. <u>Barkeeper of a club in Missouri:</u> "I prayed to God that if I should go to church in the morning, it would be a clear and nice day. It rained."
2. <u>An elderly woman in Missouri living across the street from the church:</u> "My cat is also old and not well. I cannot come until the cat dies."
3. <u>A man from Illinois:</u> "My elderly father died while sitting on the front row at church. If God would do that, I cannot attend."
4. <u>A woman to a caller:</u> "As long as I see a political sticker on a car in the parking lot, I just won't be there."
5. <u>An unhappy lady:</u> "They had a fight in that church 25 years ago."
6. <u>A non-attender:</u> "My joints hurt."
7. <u>A young man:</u> "I would go there, but he just doesn't look like a preacher."
8. <u>In 1954:</u> " He has two rear-view mirrors on his car. Preachers don't need that."
9. <u>A hard of hearing man:</u> "I can't hear a word the preacher says."
10. <u>Guilty conscience:</u> "I'm afraid you will point your finger at me. You did that once."
11. <u>A dad:</u> "I'll come when the kids are a little older."
12. <u>Father:</u> "I have to stay at home so my step-son won't steal my guns while I am in church."
13. <u>EVERYONE:</u> "It's too hot, ice cold, raining, snowing."

14. <u>Common Excuse</u> "There are rich people there and poor people looking for help. They expect you to dress up there. I won't dress to suit everybody."

15. <u>Looking hard for one:</u> "My dad was a good man and he didn't go. If he doesn't deserve heaven, no one does."

16. <u>An alcoholic:</u> "I'm too bad. You don't want me."

17. <u>Fisherman:</u> "I can worship God out on the lake."

18. <u>Past 11 years at McLeansboro, IL:</u> "The steps."

19. <u>Concerning contemporary worship:</u> "I can't stand up that long and I don't like the music."

20. <u>Typical person on the street:</u> "I am better than most church people."

21. <u>Specifically to me:</u> "I'm planning a big church wedding, and, for the pictures—nothing against YOU—but I want a taller preacher."

22. <u>The most bizarre excuse of all:</u> "I need to call on someone closer than the Lord when I need help."

Chapter 19

THE SUPERNATURAL

Much is written and discussed now about what people see and experience when they are close to death, such as angels, white light, a river of gold, etc. I have wondered if these experiences reported are hallucinations, hoaxes, or real.

Well, I can't vouch for what others say, but I can tell you from my own near-death experience I had in my life.

It all started when I woke up in the middle of the night and couldn't get my breath.

The first time this kind of thing happened I had been mowing the yard and came in to get a drink. I went to the ER and they couldn't find anything wrong with me. I went home and it happened again the next day.

I went back to the ER and they kept me overnight. About 2 in the morning, I woke up and I could not get my breath. I pressed the button for the nurse, who came down, and then I heard "Code Blue" and the room filled with people.

I thought I was going to die. I could not get my breath. I didn't want anyone to see me die. They called Kyle, my son, who is a doctor, and my chest was just heaving.

I cannot tell you the serenity, the peace, that came over me. I could see a tunnel. The nurses in the room thought I was dying, that I was going to go, and so my attending physician called the helicopter, and they flew me to Deaconness hospital in Evansville where I kept having these spells until all of a sudden they stopped and I had them no more.

That was two or three years ago, and I've not had any since. They have no medical explanation for it. When I felt that I was just about to go, I just can't tell you how peaceful it was. It was like the Lord was there with me. I have not told many people about it, for I thought they would think I was nuts.

I saw all of the nurses looking very upset and hustling about me. All of a sudden I had this enormous urge to cough which I did. I didn't cough up anything, and further evaluation and testing did not reveal a clear diagnosis. It just remember a host of people around me, hurrying and trying to do their job to help me. As I lay there wondering if I was about to do die, surprisingly I don't remember it as a bad experience.

Later I saw one of the nurses at Five Brothers who said, "I didn't expect to ever see you out here again." She thought I was having a heart attack. We laughed together about that.

With an elder in my first church who had cancer, he was expected to die any time. I went to his house. Not too long before he died, he said, "Carroll, do you want me to say hello to your brother. He's here."

In my own experience, the light was so extreme, I couldn't see anything else. In the book of Corinthians, Chapter 13, it says we see darkly now like looking into a smoky mirror but when things like this happen, we will see clearly.

Along the same almost supernatural line, I have heard many ministers and church people say that God spoke directly to them in words they could hear. That has never happened to me.

The closest I have come to this was at Jonathan Lee's funeral, July 31, 2013. When it was over and people were filing out, a man I didn't know said, "That wasn't you talking today. That was God speaking through you."

It used to bother me that God didn't speak to me. However, I remember Brother Hargrove at Lincoln said, "Don't not worry about that. Look at the talents that you have, use them, and look for an open door; don't look for God's spoken words to you." And that has been excellent advice.

In addition, I have been aware of the presence of evil: I have studied this and I have experienced it, too. Satan has a tremendous influence and temptations. The Bible speaks of besetting sin, meaning a sin that is extremely difficult to handle. These temptations are physical sometimes, such as a chemistry imbalance. All these things come together and make it very powerful.

I think that Satan has the potential to have a strong grip on everybody. We all have weaknesses. Further it might be some people have even more difficulty than others due to medical predispositions or chemical imbalances. I spent about 10 years on the local mental health board and during that time I've spoken with clinicians whose life work was treating people with mental health issues and addictions. It isn't as simple and easy as a lot of people think, but through power faith and hard work and professional help we know that Jesus is more powerful than Satan and will ultimately prevail over evil and sin.

One of the most beautiful things regarding the power of Jesus is when people work hard to develop a Christian life and overcome adversity and make it through extreme personal trials. It is truly a beautiful thing to see. Sometimes it takes a hard, long time to achieve Christian character and life perspective.

Chapter 20

FAMILY MEMBERS' PERSPECTIVE

My wife and kids have some things they want to say about me.

My Dad, Carroll Kakac

Kim Kakac Skaggs

I believe that we live in a culture today that tries to minimize fathers. I feel that I am blessed to have a great father that was an example and leader to me in my development physically, socially, and most of all spiritually.

When I was a little girl my dad made me feel so pretty and special. He would always say, "How is the prettiest girl in Fairfield?" A few years ago I told my dad how much it meant to me and that he made me feel so pretty and special and he replied "You are pretty and special." Another time when I was in college and I was discouraged about the way things were going in my life at the time and my dad said, "There is nothing that you could ever do that would make me stop loving you". I think that I have always had a great understanding of the way God loves me because of the love I felt and was shown by my dad.

I rarely saw my dad lose his temper even when my brothers and I were growing up and did things that would cause most parents to get very angry. My dad would always say before I left the house to go out growing up to remember who I was meaning that he wanted me to act like a good Christian girl and a preacher's kid. I also knew growing up when I told my dad that I was going somewhere with friends I could count on the fact that he would drive by the location and check to see if I was telling the truth. The cell phones of today held nothing over my dad's investigative powers.

Christmas at our home growing up was a very special time and my favorite time of the year. We always had lots of Christmas decorations and presents. Dad always read the Christmas story on Christmas Eve every year and then we opened Christmas gifts. We always had big birthday celebrations for our birthdays as well and dad would pray a special blessing over us before the party. We still read the Christmas story from the Bible on Christmas and dad still prays a birthday prayer before the family's birthday parties.

When I was growing up, another memory that is great is going to Oil Belt Camp with my dad as the Dean of the week. I remember all the kids loving dad and he loved the camp atmosphere and camaraderie as well. Dad has a great sense of humor and he enjoyed all the pranks and fun of church camp.

When I got married, I felt very nervous right before the ceremony but I felt that all was going to be fine when dad walked me down the aisle toward my husband-to-be. All felt right with my world on my dad's arm walking to a new future with my husband.

When I started dating, I was talking to my dad about what qualities I would like to have in a husband. My dad said, "You need to think about what you have to offer as a wife and give to a relationship instead of what you can get from someone else." My dad always said that marriage is not 50/50. He said sometimes it is 90/10 and sometimes 20/80 as one partner picks the other one up when they need help. I have never heard my parents have an argument in front of me. I know that they did disagree about things sometimes but they always backed each other in front of me and my brothers.

One of my earliest memories of my dad is going to his office at the church with him and playing quietly while he worked. We all sat at the table almost every night for supper and we would take turns reading a short devotion and prayer before eating. My dad believed in table manners and we were gently reprimanded if we did not use good manners.

My dad loves watching sports on TV and also going to local Mules sporting events. I can remember my dad lying on the couch on Sunday after church watching Wrestling at the Chase on KPLR TV and laughing.

My dad was and still is a huge St. Louis Cardinals and Fairfield Mules fan. We had one TV when I was growing up and dad liked to watch Hee Haw on Saturday night. On Saturday night I remember he usually would get a phone call from his good friend Charlie Mitchell who would call just to touch base with dad.

I have always felt shy about talking to people and my dad was trying to help me. Dad said, "When you are shy you are selfish because you are thinking about yourself and what other people are thinking about you. You need to become genuinely interested in other people and then you won't be shy." My dad is so interested in other people and I have seen him help so many people throughout the years. My dad has never had a lot of money but what he has he gives to other people.

I believe that my dad has never felt that being a minister was a job; to him it is a calling. Many times when I was growing up dad would make plans with the family and at the last minute someone in the congregation would pass away and the trip would be cancelled. My dad never showed any anger or disappointment at the disruption of his plans. I never saw my dad ever curse, smoke or drink and he always has just kept serving the Lord during his whole life. Dad only misses a church service if he is ill and he still is serving the Lord as a minister.

I remember our house always being a home where I was welcome at any time. I always think of asking my dad for advice now about things in my life and his grandkids also feel that they can ask him advice as well. When I go to dad's house now it still feels like home and he makes all his family feel welcome at any time. My dad has always loved jokes, laughter, telling stories and being around people.

When my dad found out that he had cancer a few years ago he came to tell me about the diagnosis. I was crying and distraught and my dad just quietly prayed with me that I would be able to be comforted and accept God's will about the cancer. He was comforting me instead of my comforting him with his diagnosis. Dad went through the cancer treatment experience with grace and dignity.

My dad taught me the love of a father and made me feel loved and safe throughout my life. He taught me what it means to be a Christian and I will be forever grateful for his example.

Carroll Kakac, My Dad

Kevin Kakac

Contrary to my mother's belief and suspicions, ever since Steve asked me to write a few words for this book – I have on many occasions contemplated and stewed over just what to put down on paper. Of course only the best writers of biography are able to capture, in a highly readable way, the essence of the character about whom they are writing. I needed to remind myself that not only am I not a talented writer – but that what Steve asked me to do was just put a few thoughts down… not write the book.

To me, the trick when writing about someone else - is to find a way to mentally take a step back and objectify the subject material. Not an easy task for me when the subject matter is my father. This is especially true because many of the most interesting, poignant and meaningful stories and anecdotes within a family - are also typically of the most intimate and personal sort – those which either don't belong in a published book – or even if they would be highly interesting – inclusion or reference would likely get me the cold shoulder at family get togethers for many years to come – or worse. So with these caveats stated, the following are some thoughts I hope my dad – and any reader of this book will find enlightening.

A big part of any individual's character is established by the circumstances into which he was born. Dad is no exception. As a farm kid in the 1930s and 1940s in Iowa, dad grew up working hard on the farm with multi-generations of his family. His family worked hard and for long hours within a community of other people that worked hard and long hours. To be busy and industrious and involved in one's work was ingrained in dad from a very young age – and in the farming context – the work is not only self-defining – it was and remains today a way of life. Farming for a living has no set hours per week and dad takes that same mental approach toward his ministry. He just does what needs to be done in a timely fashion – when it needs to be done.

Growing up we often tended to compare our dad's 'work hours' with other friends dads' and noted that ours 'worked' all weekends, most week nights and other various and sundry times at which time most are 'off duty'. However, dad never did and still doesn't see his ministry as work, or as a job. He is a person who has become a professional - who has answered a call – a call to the ministry. One of his favorite sayings about the many hours he spends in carrying the duties and responsibilities of his ministry is that, "…Sunday keeps coming whether you're ready or not…" - ever the reminder that a big portion of my dad's work falls on all 52 weeks of every year. No exceptions.

Dad often says he highly enjoyed the vigorous farming life and came within a hair's breadth of becoming a farmer after high school. Dad's family were highly respected farmers and had a fair amount of acreage to manage. Meanwhile, his surviving brothers showed no interest in helping out with the farming activities. At around this time dad's maternal grandmother offered to set him up on the family farm in Iowa. After much thought and (I imagine) prayer, he decided that he would follow the path to the ministry. Although dad still enjoys driving through the fields at various times of the year to observe farming activities – and joking with his many friends in farming – I know he has no regrets about his decision to become a minister. I think one goal though - that dad still aspires to - and that has remained out of his reach – is the coveted "Honorary Mill Shoals Farmer" certificate that so few have received – but so many desire. (If he has received this in recent years – I know it to be one of his most cherished accomplishments!)

I mention dad's farming background because he brought the work ethic that was ingrained in him on the farm to his duties and responsibilities as a minister. You've heard many say find a job that you love and you'll never work a day in your life? I have often thought that this phrase aptly describes my dad's attitude and devotion to his duties as a minister.

What has made dad such a good fit for the job of minister over the year is that he loves and believes in the Lord and the way of life provided by the Christianity. Additionally, dad always says that to the extent he has been able to be successful as a minister in the churches in which he as served, he believes that it is in no small part tied to his desire and willingness to engage in social interaction and discourse not only with church members – but members of the community in which the church is located. Perhaps put more plainly, dad always enjoys heading to wherever the largest group of folks are – usually the coffee shop/restaurant – and mixing up with church-goers and non-church goers alike. In this way, dad has often told me he is able to reach and interact with far more people for the Lord - as well as continue to make new and interesting friends. Often these friendships have lasted decades. Sometimes, through no calculated plan of my dad's, some of these friends have no doubt seen something in dad that led them to become regular church-goers as well. Dad has an innate intelligence and curiosity about people and events – and just genuinely likes and enjoys being around and with people of all sorts – wherever he goes. This is a very desirable characteristic for a minister to possess – especially when it comes naturally. A good sense of humor and basic optimism helps as well – and dad has always possessed these traits in over abundance.

While no person is perfect and dad would be the first to say he is no exception, his success in the ministry has been greatly assisted over the years by his authenticity and personal integrity. As a minister dad has always done a great job of living the Christian example and preaching it every chance he gets. In this way he lives what he preaches and preaches what he lives – and therein comes the authenticity. On a personal level – dad's authenticity serves as a guiding light and daily inspiration to his entire family. Thanks for everything, dad. Keep up the good work.

Carroll Kakac, My Father

Kyle Kakac

"Above all things love one another." I Peter 4:8

I always tell people my goal is to be "half the man my father is." If I accomplish that, I will feel pretty satisfied. I realize now that my father is not a wealthy man, but he and my mother created a very spiritually rich environment for our family and I never remember wanting for anything. We overlook the warts of life as we grow more removed from them by time, and I know it is an oversimplification, but I look back on my childhood as a rather idyllic one. As a parent myself now I realize that "idyllic childhoods" do not happen by chance and are instead a byproduct of fate and very good parenting.

If there was one defining characteristic my father possesses I would say that it is a seemingly boundless love of others. As a child I always remember feeling this powerful love. One could just feel it, plus he tells us he loves us all the time as well. I clearly remember feeling this same love in my father directed towards the other members of our family, his friends, the members of our church family, and just people randomly, anywhere.

My mother always loved to go to the shopping malls when I was a child, something that I have to admit my father probably does NOT love. But because he loves my mother we would frequently go to a shopping mall after my father finished visiting someone in his congregation in a hospital in St Louis or Evansville. Dad would just pick out a bench somewhere and strike up conversations with other men waiting for their wives. I would always be amazed at the things he would get these random strangers to tell him in the short time he would be with them. But I think these strangers told these sometimes intimate details to him because they, too, immediately sensed that my father loved and cared about them.

Dad has always had a great sense of humor. I remember every Saturday night his buddy Charlie Mitchell would call him and tell him a joke. It was a routine of their long friendship. I never heard the actual jokes or him recount them to my mother because I was in bed by the time Charlie always called, but I still remember the booming laughter regularly elicited.

Dad likes to watch rather silly shows on television. Shows that might surprise people like "Mama's Family" and "Married with Children" come to mind. He also loves to watch his beloved St Louis Cardinals.

A couple of funny stories always come to mind with regard to my Dad. One was the time he was showing my brother and I the "safe" way to light off firecrackers. He was attempting to light a firecracker in his hand with a match when he accidentally dropped the match between his legs on top of an entire 1000 count brick of firecrackers setting off the entire bunch. I've never seen, before or since, my dad move with such athletic prowess and agility, rolling and flipping and running away from that fusillade.

Another time Dad and my brother and I were at Frank Walter's place on Sunset Lake and Dad decided to show us the "safe" way to get into a canoe off of a dock. As soon as he placed his second foot into the canoe, we could tell it was all over. Let us just say that balance was never achieved and he ended up on his hands and knees in 2 foot of water without his glasses with a quite comical expression on his face. It took a long time for the laughter to cease that day, including Dad laughing at himself, something he has always felt comfortable doing.

Dad has always enjoyed going to the local coffee shops. As long as I can remember he has eaten breakfast there every morning, taken a mid morning coffee, and also a mid afternoon coffee. To some that would seem like quite a bit of coffee, but I feel like he thought of it as an opportunity to "get out amongst the flock." Further I think he, again, just really loves people and loves to fellowship and socialize with them. In small towns like Fairfield, the coffee shops are the nerve centers of the community and accordingly an important place for a community minded preacher to spend a great deal of time. I am certain it has benefited his ministry over the years.

Another funny thing I think about in relation to my Dad is his dedication to nap taking. When looking at our albums of family pictures over the years, in about 40% of the pictures my Dad is either taking a nap or is laying down on the couch looking like he just woke up from one. My dad tells me it is a habit born of growing up on the farm in Iowa where the the boys and men woke up very early to work hard at chores, etc. They would work hard all morning, eat lunch and then everyone would take a nap during the hot part of the day before going back to work again in the afternoon. He tells me he has done that his entire life, even after the farm work ceased. He is a world class sleeper…he can sleep in any circumstance, position, etc.….As an adult I realize this is in fact a gift which is actually quite rare. I think more people would benefit from taking more naps. The world would be a better place.

In summary, I honestly could not have hoped for a better father. He loved his family immensely and provided a very nurturing environment for us. He showed us by example how to love and serve others. He is a great example of a life well lived…a demonstration that the key to fulfillment and meaningfulness in life is a life of service to others, with humility, humor and grace.

Carroll Kakac, My Husband

Karen Kakac

The first time I met Carroll Kakac was when he was a student minister and was preaching a revival at my home church in Atlanta, Missouri. He and our minister, Harold Boldon, came to the home of my parents, Gerald and Aldena Corbin, for a meal. My dad was an elder in the church and often invited the minister for meals, to fish, hunt, etc. I was too young to date, but I recall thinking that Carroll was cute!

Not too many years later, we met again at White Oak Christian Service Camp in Moberly, Missouri. I was a senior in high school, and he was the young student minister of the Benton City Christian Church and was on the camp faculty. We spent quite a bit of time together and he asked me for a date a few weeks later. On our first date we went to a revival meeting and, after dating four years and being married nearly 55 years, we are still going to church together!

Carroll and I were married on September 22, 1961 at my home church in Atlanta by Carroll's brother-in-law, Harlan Williams. Carroll's youngest brother, Don Kakac, was the best man, and his older brother, Fillmore Kakac, and Howard Merchant were groomsmen. My cousin, Nova Roan Merchant, was my matron of honor and bridesmaids were Pat Robison Ferguson and Janice Farmer Peterson. The weather was terrible! There were earthshaking crashes of thunder and lightening when the guests were arriving, during, and after the ceremony! We jokingly say that our marriage started off very stormy, but has managed to survive all these years!

At the time of our wedding Carroll was the minister at Novelty, Missouri. During his ministry there, the church grew to become larger than the population of the small town. The church purchased and remodeled a parsonage for us, and our first child, Kim, was born while we were there. Those were the days before disposable diapers, so we had to drive 10 miles to the nearest laundrymat because we had no washer or dryer. Also, we only had one car until several years after we moved to Illinois.

First Christian Church, in Shelbina, Missouri, called Carroll to be their minister in 1963 and he served there for nearly eight years. During this period of time the church officially departed from the Disciples of Christ organization and became an independent Christian church, a missionary program was established, and an evening service was started. Our son, Kevin, was born while we were living in Shelbina. He had some serious health issues and was hospitalized many times. The church people and the community were extremely good to us and those acts of kindness will never be forgotten.

We moved to Fairfield, Illinois, the day after Thanksgiving in 1970 where Carroll became the senior minister at First Christian Church and served for nearly 34 years. A few of the accomplishments during this time include a new parsonage built for the senior minister's family, the previous parsonage remodeled for the youth minister, a children's minister and music minister were added to the staff, and preschool and latchkey programs were established. The church attendance greatly increased and an additional morning service was added, while still holding the well-attended Sunday night and Wednesday night services. Our youngest son, Kyle, was born in Fairfield.

When Steve asked me to write my thoughts in his book about our family, specifically about my husband, I was hesitant because I wasn't sure what to include. I decided to write about the characteristics that I have observed throughout our many years together. When it comes to Carroll's life there is nothing pretentious. He is like an open book - what you see is what you get! FRIENDLY, FAMILY-ORIENTED, PATIENT, KIND, HAPPY, INVOLVED, FAITHFUL, DEDICATED, and LOVING.

FRIENDLY - One of the first things that impressed me about Carroll was his friendliness and how easy it was to talk to him. That is still true today, as he truly loves people and is interested in them. We often joke about his "coffee ministry" at the local restaurant. Every morning at 7:00 a.m., many retired men would enjoy "sleeping in," but Carroll is like a little boy who can't wait to see his friends and help them solve the world's problems over a cup of brew at Five Brothers or one of the local restaurants.

Shopping is not one of Carroll's favorite things, but occasionally he will go with me. He considers it his job to sit in the mall on a bench and wait until I return so we can go eat. Almost always, he will be talking to strangers he just met and will know all about them, their family, jobs, and interests. He especially loves to talk about his Lord and the church to anyone who will listen.

FAMILY ORIENTED – Carroll's biggest goal in life is that all of his children and grandchildren become Christians and live according the God's plan found in the Bible. We are indeed blessed to have all of our family faithful and involved in church work. He feels that this is his greatest heritage.

The Fairfield church encouraged Carroll to attend the North American Christian Convention each year and, for several years, they paid the expenses for our family to attend. It was such an inspirational time for all of us to hear the great singing and preaching, attend workshops, and join with the thousands of other Christians from all over the world. Our children loved kiddieland, the children's and teen activities, and we will always have good memories of those trips together.

We have had the privilege of hosting hundreds of church members, visiting missionaries, ministers, evangelists, college and musical groups. This has been a wonderful blessing, especially for our children as they were exposed to many various personalities and cultures right in their own home. One of the most unusual visits that I recall was when we had three missionaries visiting from Poland who could not speak a word of English and, of course, we couldn't speak their language either. They were to meet the American missionary speaker at our house, but he didn't arrive until 3-4 hours later! Somehow, we managed to communicate and it was memorable experience for all of us.

Family birthdays are important and we always try to get together to celebrate each one with a special meal/party if time and distance allows. These meals range from a huge dinner or barbecue to one of our all-time favorites – pizza from DiMaggios!

A favorite family tradition is at Christmas time, usually on Christmas Eve, when our family gathers together to celebrate our Savior's birth. We have a big holiday meal, then gather around the Christmas tree and read the Christmas story from Luke 2. In years past Carroll was always the reader but now, due to his fading eyesight, one of the younger family members does the reading. After the scripture reading and prayer we open our gifts. It is a special time for all of us.

PATIENT - Not many people in today's world have the "patience of Job" mentioned in the Bible, but I believe that Carroll is one who exhibits that characteristic in his everyday life. No matter what is on his personal agenda, he is always willing to take the time necessary to listen and counsel those who come to him to get solutions to their problems. In his own life, he does not rush into decisions but has the faith to wait for God's guidance. Everyone in this world has problems at times, and our family is no exception; however, we always try to remember that God is in control. We prayerfully ask for God's help and He gives it.

Patience is probably one of the keys to his long ministries. Carroll is willing to wait and allow the church board members to make decisions rather than try to push his own ideas forward. The Bible teaches that the elders are the overseers of the church and we are to follow them in carrying out God's plans.

I do recall one example when his patience was severely tested. Kevin was in college and had a summer law internship in Mississippi. He invited us down to visit him and then go on to New Orleans. Having never been to that city, we decided to do it. I made the hotel reservations and when we arrived we discovered it was in a "less than ideal" location in the French Quarter. With no other hotels available, Carroll asked at the check-in desk where to park our car and parked it as instructed. After unpacking and getting settled into our room, we set out walking to see the sights and were gone until about 10:00 p.m. Much of the late-night entertainment was a disappointment and not what we had expected. On our return to the hotel, we noticed our car was missing! Checking at the desk, Carroll was told that we had parked in a no parking zone and our car had been towed! He tried to explain to the new desk clerk that he had only followed the instruction he'd been given earlier, but it fell on deaf ears. We ended up taking a taxi across the city to claim our car and paying a large fine to retrieve it. Carroll was as exasperated as I've ever seen him. He said he wouldn't stay in that city another hour, so we returned to the hotel, packed up our belongings and drove to another town to spend the night. He vowed to never go back to New Orleans, and when we got home he wrote a letter to the mayor of the city with his complaint and requested his money be refunded. The letter was not answered, of course, and it may have been the last time I made the hotel reservations . . . .

KIND – Carroll would never do anything to intentionally hurt anyone's feelings. He sometimes agonizes over things he's said in his sermons that might have offended anyone, and this is not always easy when you preach the Bible truths. In a public setting, he is the type person who searches out some individual who is sitting alone and starts up a conversation with him or her. He definitely does not exclude anyone or try to climb the "social ladder". This makes him appealing to people in all walks of life. He is a person who looks at glass of water as half full, not half empty, and he expects the best from people.

When Carroll was the minister at Fairfield he was able to provide help to many transients and people in need. The church had a special fund, largely due to the donations of an anonymous church member, that was specifically to be used for people that he deemed needy, and many people were helped in this way. Some criticism was received that perhaps some were given help that really were not worthy. This was probably true in some cases as Carroll has a big heart. He always said he'd rather help someone who didn't really need it than to turn away anyone who did. God would be the ultimate judge in such matters.

HAPPY – A cheerful, upbeat personality is definitely one of Carroll's good attributes. He certainly enjoys a good laugh – even if the joke is on him.

One Saturday before Easter, Carroll was in his office reviewing his sermon for Easter Sunday morning. Somehow, without him noticing, it fell off his desk and into the wastebasket! The janitor, unknowingly, emptied the trash into the dumpster in the back alley behind the church. When Carroll couldn't find his sermon, he realized what must have happened, so he decided to try to retrieve it from the trash. He always writes his sermons out by hand so had no backup in the computer. The large trash container was quite tall and Carroll is short, but he was determined. He somehow was able to climb up into the container and was able to find his sermon. However, the hard part was getting out! The ladder had slipped down and he was trapped. He began to yell as loudly as he could from inside the trash container. He waved at people and they waved back and went on by in their cars. Finally, a little boy was walking through the alley and heard him and asked him what he was doing in the trash container. He put the ladder back up so Carroll was able to crawl out. The local newspaper printed the story, as did the Evansville paper and others nationwide!

When other people realize you have a good sense of humor they are more likely to play jokes. Our front yard along the street had been plowed up and had been without grass for many weeks due to the city working on an unfinished sewer problem. People were beginning to notice the mess and were commenting on it. One day we noticed some plants coming up!

As they grew taller and larger, Carroll recognized them as turnips growing in our front yard! He never found out for sure who planted them, but suspected it was either his neighbor or some of his "coffee buddies" who had planted them as a prank!

INVOLVED –In addition to preaching for more than 63 years, Carroll has always enjoyed being active in the community where he lived, as well as witnessing all over the world. Although he seldom mentions them, his honors and accomplishments are many and varied. They include the usual ministerial duties such as teaching classes, speaking at various church and community events, revivals, and conducting hundreds of weddings and funerals.

The Fairfield church is widely known throughout the world for its effective and inclusive missionary program that grew under Carroll's leadership from $36,500 in 1970 to a yearly budget of over $200,000 at his retirement in 2004. For a small town of 6,000 people this was a remarkable accomplishment! More importantly, today the church still continues to increase its giving.

One of the highlights of his ministry was preaching and teaching on an African mission trip in 1976. Carroll has served on the Polish Mission Board, Fellowship of the American Medical Evangelism Board(FAME), Christian Church Foundation for the Handicapped Board(Knoxville, TN) Board, and was president of the Zambia Christian Mission Board.

In addition, he was on the White Oak, Shelby County, and Oil Belt Christian Service Camp boards, and served as trustee at Central Christian College of the Bible and Lincoln Christian College. He helped organize the Southern Illinois Christian Convention and was president; served several terms on the North American Christian Convention Committee, and was National Prayer Chairman. He was also on the National Missionary Convention Committee and has presented many workshops at both of our national conventions. In the year 2000, at the North American Christian Convention at Louisville, Kentucky, he was presented the Lincoln Christian College Distinguished Alumni Award.

Growing up in a patriotic family and having served in the Army National Guard, Carroll was frequently asked to speak at Memorial and Veterans Day services and was always willing to comply. He has been active in many community activities throughout the years such as the

Rotary Club, Lions Club, Ministerial Alliance, Hospital Chaplain, Red Cross Blood Drive Chairman, Masonic Lodge, a speaker on a weekly radio program, and was treasurer of the Wayne County 708 Mental Health Board. He was selected as "Man of the Year" by the Fairfield Woman's Club, received the Modern Woodman of the World Award, and was chosen to be Grand Marshal of the Fairfield Merchants Christmas parade.

An avid sports enthusiast, he supports the local athletic boosters' clubs, Colt Backers and Mulebackers, and is regularly seen attending sporting events, especially, when his children or grandchildren are participants!

On his retirement from the Fairfield Church in 2004, Mayor Mickey Borah proclaimed a "Carroll Kakac Day" and a reception was held and attended by a large number of friends and people from the community, as well as the congregation. The Fairfield church established a $1,000 scholarship in his honor at Lincoln Christian College that is being used to train young ministers to preach the Gospel.

Many in today's world seek recognition and power in their lives, but Carroll avoids personal praise and gives all of the glory to God for anything that he may have accomplished. He is also grateful to all of the wonderful Christian people that he has had the privilege to work with throughout the years.

FAITHFUL – From the very beginning of our lives together, Carroll made it very clear that Jesus Christ must have first place in his life. When all my friends were having dates on Saturday nights, Carroll told me he stayed at home and went to bed early so he would be prepared for the Lord's Day on Sunday. After we were married, there were numerous convention plans and vacations that had to be cancelled at the last minute because someone in the congregation needed him for a funeral or a serious problem arose. I made the necessary adjustments in my life and we BOTH put Jesus Christ first in our lives and served Him together!

DEDICATED - Carroll believes in worshipping God and participating in the Lord's Supper every Sunday. He takes it seriously where the scripture says, "Do not forsake the assembling of yourselves together" and "They met on the first day of the week to break bread". Many times he has taken communion to shut-ins and those unable to be in the church service. Even if the weather was terrible, he never wanted to cancel church for any reason, and seldom did unless the elders insisted on it. When church was cancelled, our family always read the scriptures and observed the communion service at home. Carroll always wanted to attend any meetings or social events where he "could do some good" for the Lord.

After his retirement from the Fairfield church in 2004, Carroll was not satisfied to simply be an "in the pew" church member. When he had an opportunity to become the minister in a small church at McLeansboro, Illinois, he returned to preaching every Sunday and loves doing it. For more than 45 years he has been a leader in a weekly prayer breakfast that includes men from the church and the community. He continues to conduct funerals and weddings, and has preached revivals every year since 2005 at the Ashland Christian Church. Through the years he has had some serious health issues, including diabetes and colon cancer, but he says that you cannot retire from serving God and, at 87 years of age, he has no plans to stop!

LOVING – This is the real reason that Carroll's life has been successful. He loves God, his family, his fellowman and he has no reservations about doing everything possible to make this world a better place. He believes that people come to church to learn about God and His plan of salvation, and that they want to hear it preached. His ultimate goal is to prepare all of us for everlasting life in heaven.

Chapter 21

MY LEGACY

When my life is ended, I hope to leave behind a legacy. The following are a few general comments worth sharing.

First, my favorite hymn is "Amazing Grace," which I want sung at my funeral. The man who wrote the hymn was far away from God in the slave trade business, became a Christian, and then wrote the hymn "Amazing Grace" that could forgive a person like him.

I haven't had his lifestyle or anything like that, but I still think that the greatest miracle that there is in this world is where God can take a person and save him. And then, I just like to hear this song; it makes me feel good. It's my favorite song. I'm not a great musician, but this is a song that is meaningful to me.

How did I want to be remembered? I want to be remembered by people as a real person, not somebody who was putting on a show or trying to be someone he was not. I'd rather be remembered as a person who tried to live by what God has told me about how to live. I can't be remembered as many preachers are remembered.

To me, one of the most significant scriptures is Romans 1: 16, which has always been my favorite: "For I'm not ashamed of the gospel of Jesus Christ," and that's what I have lived by. Also, John 3: 16: "For God so loved the world that He gave His only begotten Son, that whosoever should believe on Him should not perish but have everlasting life." Both of these scriptures kind of sum up what it's all about.

Most ministers shy away from the book of Revelation because they haven't taken the time to understand it for what it really is. I think there are a lot of things in the Bible we are not meant to understand right now, but when the time comes, we will. But the time will come when we will see clearly. The things that we understand are easy to understand in the Book of Revelation. But with the other parts of it I think when the time comes, we'll know.

Because I'm not a talented person, I have to be personable with people. That is my strongest ability as a minister. Also, I don't have to be that—I enjoy doing that. If I had it all to do over, I think I would do more coffee shops, because there you meet the people of the community and you get the heartbeat of the community out there. Most of the people I drink coffee with are members of the church, but once in a while you get someone who isn't. What some ministers consider a waste of time, I consider my strong point.

In order for the minister to know the pulse of the community, he must be IN the community, be a part of it. I was always taught that, as much as possible, I should participate in community things because that's the only way to know what people think and do. Although God has never spoken direct words to me, as I have read His Word most every day, sometimes it directly speaks to me as to something I am trying to decide.

Why have I not retired? Actually, I don't know how to do anything else. When the McLeansboro church was talking of closing, and they asked me to help them out. I've been there now 12 years. When did God tell us to retire from His work anyway? And speaking of McLeansboro, the church I am in now has given me a time of peace, perfect peace. I attend no board meetings, I just preach, and I let them handle the administration of the congregation.

The most enjoyable time in my whole life was when our children were all home. They all did well, and it was exciting.

My most prized possessions are my Bible and my family.

My favorites include Five Brothers Restaurant, steak, chocolate, lemon pie, roses, the Christian Standard, Snoopy, and notes in my Bible from my kids and grandkids.

Why do people hold the minister up to higher standards than they themselves have? It's true that they do, and people who are outside the church and don't understand it at all are especially that way. They feel, "Well, you are a preacher; you shouldn't become angry, etc."

I think that there is a sense of right and wrong in the worst of us, and it takes a person who is trying to do what's right to appeal to that. It's true in all civilizations.

If people don't know the true and living God, they worship something, like a volcano, the sun, etc. They feel the need to worship something that is greater than they are. All people are born to have that desire to get to the truth about life. That's one of the advantages that we have in evangelism that the church doesn't realize today. People expect ministers to do better than they do.

It's like the old joke of a mother giving her boy advice as he was going into the Army: telling him it was going to be difficult and all that morally. When he got back, she asked him how he got along, and he said I got along fine, they never did know I was a Christian.

I don't have many fears, but I do fear losing my sermon. I write my sermons out or I wouldn't say the right thing. One Sunday in McLeansboro, I left my sermon at home, and had to resort to the 23rd Psalm, which is pretty well organized into parts itself.

Without notes, you run on and on. They used to say, "If you want to preach 20 minutes, study and write it out, and if you want preach an hour and a half, just don't worry about it." I have a fear of not doing what God expects me to do. I have a fear of being misinterpreted as I talk to people. I have never been confident about my own talents. At the first of my ministry, I asked God to give me a small church in the Ozark mountains and that would be good enough for me. That didn't happen.

I don't think I view myself as others view me. The first time I heard a sermon on a recorder, I could not believe it was me.

I have sometimes had the most positive comments on a sermon I thought was not good; sometimes negative, in a sermon I thought was excellent.

Needless to say, in this book it was impossible to mention all the wonderful people who have been my friends throughout the years. The congregations that I served and the good Christian workers therein certainly share the credit for any success I was able to attain. Of course, the real glory goes to God!

I'd like to personally thank Steven Lee, the author of this book, for his idea to write a book regarding my life. It is very humbling to know that he was interested and cared enough to attempt such a task.

It took Steve about three years to assemble the information he needed. He interviewed me weekly for several months, giving me questionnaires to fill out with information about my life and the churches I served, and asking pertinent questions that he thought might reveal incidents of interest to his readers.

During the writing of this book, Steve experienced personal tragedy within his own life, and his tireless commitment to this project in the face of hardship makes us all the more grateful for dedication to telling this story.

Thank you, Steve.

Afterword

Just as launching this book seemed like a formidable task because of the stature and magnitude of service Carroll Kakac has lived, so, likewise it if difficult to conclude it for the same reasons.

How do I end something that has not ended?

I have decided to wrap this up by writing about what has impressed me the most about Carroll's character.

Carroll loves the great old hymns of the church, the ones that have stood the test of time. Not musical himself, he loves music.

His dress code has been consistent for more than 60 years: suit, white shirt, tie, and dress shoes. He does not vary in this, thinking that people should dress their best when they come into the House of God, showing their respect and reverence. A personal appearance, he thinks, speaks of the bond between man and God. People should give their best to God and not be slovenly.

When delivering a sermon, Carroll makes each individual in the congregation feel as if he is looking directly at him or her. His skill for eye contact is phenomenal as he speaks from notes that he has carefully prepared and rehearsed.

What a voice Carroll has. Even though he says he has been embarrassed by listening to a recording of himself, his tone is pleasing, mellow, clear, and memorable. While you have been reading this book, if you have listened to his sermons, you have probably been able to hear him, in your head, speak the words.

It is a rare person who feels comfortable with people wherever he is. That is Carroll, who can meet people from all walks of life, talk to them effortlessly, and make them know that he is interested in them and cares about them. Waving to people while driving through town, he never seems to meet a stranger.

The ruination and downfall and dismissal of many preachers has come from closely bonding to a few people in the church, and making it clear that everyone else is excluded from that closeness.

I think part of Carroll's longevity at his churches has been due to the fact that he did not become part of an exclusive clique. As a result, people felt equal with Carroll and did not resent his taking up with a chosen few people. He can stop to talk to anyone, asking, "How are you?" and mean it sincerely. He has time for people.

Another strength Carroll has is in his sermon delivery. He does not believe in theatrics and charisma as a means to get a message across. Instead, he stands still and tells the Gospel message, seeing no need to jump, dance, yell, or get red in the face. He is a real person, not an actor playing a part on a stage.

In today's world, dependability is a precious commodity. In the 34 years that Carroll was minister to the Fairfield congregation, he was always there. His weekly pulpit appointment was almost never broken. When he was not there, which only happened twice that I remember, there was a general alarm, knowing that he had a serious illness that prevented his presence. I always firmly believed that he wanted to be there, no matter what was happening in his life, and that only a hospital bed kept him away.

Finally, I turn to Geoffrey Chaucer's Canterbury Tales, which I taught for many years at Flora High School. In the Prologue, a description is given of a humble Parson. In the margin of my teacher's book, I wrote by this paragraph, "Carroll Kakac," for it sums up a Christian man of unshakeable integrity:

"I think there never was a better priest.
He had no thirst for pomp and ceremony,
Nor spiced his conscience and morality,
But Christ's own law, and His apostle's twelve he taught,
But first he followed it himself."

Steven Lee
February 9, 2017

Anna Popelka & & Thomas Kakac 11
Thomas Kakac 1 &J-2-(2)

Carroll's great-grandparents, seated, Anna Popelka and Thomas John Kakac, emigrated from Czechoslovakia to the United States. They named their two sons Thomas John (left) and John Thomas (right, Carroll's grandfather). Anna died in her fifties. Thomas went back to Czechoslovakia for a bride, leaving his two sons to farm. Thomas married Elizabeth Podfreznick, who was younger than his sons, "a very poor person with a son," and returned to Saratoga, Iowa. His sons did not expect him to return from Czechoslovakia. Thomas John (son) and John Thomas had claimed the family country store and farm, respectively. Consequently, at age 65, Thomas John, the father, started a family with Elizabeth in Hogan, Wisconsin, farming and having 5 more children, 1 boy and 4 girls. Thomas John, the father, never again contacted his sons in Saratoga, Iowa. After Carroll came to Fairfield, IL, two old ladies came to his office, speaking Czech, and identified themselves as Thomas John's two daughters from his second family in Wisconsin.

Kakac Cousins: (front, from left) Lowell, David, Janice,
Jim Davis, (back) Carroll, Victor, and Fillmore.

Victor and Blanche Kakac, their wedding picture, 1920's.

Kakac Siblings: Fillmore and Don (top) Janice and Carroll.

Guess Who?

Pictured is Carroll C. Kakac, former longtime minister at Fairfield's First Christian Church. Kakac is still ministering in the area. The picture was taken while he was in the pulpit at his first full-time ministry in Benton City, Missouri in 1952.

Guess Who?

Does anyone recognize this well-known minister who is still a full time preacher in the area?

Township offers a $300 reward for apprehension and conviction of those responsible for putting sugar into a road grader fuel tank . . . Loren Harris, bookkeeper for the Bernard Podolsky oil engineering office, is

Carroll as a young minister at Benton City, MO.

Karen and Carroll's wedding picture.

The Kakac family in 1973: Karen holding Kyle, Kevin, Kim, and Carroll.

Kakacs to Celebrate 50th Wedding Anniversary

Carroll and Karen (Corbin) Kakac, 18 Park Lane, Fairfield, Illinois, will celebrate their 50th wedding anniversary on September 22, 2011.

They were married at First Christian Church in Atlanta, on September 22, 1961, by Carroll's brother-in-law, Harlan Williams. Carroll's younger brother, Don Kakac, was his best man; his older brother, Fillmore Kakac, and a college friend, Howard Merchant, were groomsmen. Karen's cousin, Nova (Roan) Merchant, was matron of honor; and friends of the bride, Janice (Farmer) Peterson and Pat (Robison) Ferguson were bridesmaids.

Carroll was born in Cresco, Iowa, and graduated from Missouri Valley High School. After serving in the Army National Guard, Carroll graduated from Lincoln Bible Institute(now Lincoln University) in Lincoln, Illinois. He began preaching his first year in college and has been a minister for 59 years. He ministered for Christian churches in Benton City, Novelty, and Shelbina, before moving to Fairfield, Ill., in 1970, where he was the senior minister at First Christian Church for 33½ years. At the present time, he is the minister of First Christian Church in McLeansboro, Ill.

Karen was born in Atlanta, Missouri, and graduated from

Mr. and Mrs. Carroll Kakac

Missouri, for three years, and, later, graduated from Eastern Illinois University. For the past 30 years, she has been employed at Fairfield Community High School.

The Kakacs have three children who all live in Fairfield: Kim Skaggs (Doug), WIC Coordinator/Nurse at Wayne Co. Health Department; Kev-

in Kakac (Sharmila), Legal Counsel for Peoples National Bank; and Dr. Kyle Kakac (Amanda), Primary Care Physician at Horizon Health Care. They have five grandchildren: Victor Skaggs, Corbin, Ethan and Claire Kakac, and Caroline Kakac.

A family celebration will be held at a later date.

Carroll and Karen celebrate their fiftieth anniversary.

94

Kakac brothers today: Carroll, Fillmore, and Don.

Carroll's family today: (seated, from left) Caroline, Carroll, Bo, Karen, Claire, (standing, from left) Doug, Kim, Victor, Kyle, Amanda, Sharmila, Corbin, Kevin, and Ethan.

Printed in the United States
By Bookmasters